#1 book for fixing
Read Before Marriage and/or Divorce.

Free Prenuptial Agreement Enclosed. Colonel Smoke is a genius when it comes to women, and is fixing marriages and relationships every day. I cherish all women. I want to help them become a nicer person, says Colonel Smoke, "The Master".

All Men Are Stupid

is the opinion of most American women?

101 Guaranteed Ways to a Happy Relationship with the one you love.

 This is an Instruction manual for both men and women. This manuscript (counselor's edition), teaches men and women how to communicate with each other every day, and will explain what's expected from one another in the 21st century.

Copyright © 2014 Authored by Colonel B.S. Smoke
All rights reserved. AAAAA

ISBN: 1540494101
ISBN 13: 978-1540494108
Library of Congress Control Number: XXXXX (If applicable)
LCCN Imprint Name: City and State (If applicable)

INTRODUCTION

This book, *"All Men Are Stupid" is* a must read for both men and women. It is written to teach men all about the irrational and emotional behavior of women in the 21st Century. The manuscript is about freeing yourself from women whose sole purpose in life is to be nasty, ungrateful, and disrespectful to their man. Ladies, we got it. No problem! Men remember, you always have to be respectful and nice to your lady if she is kind, loveable and deserves it. That was easy.

This manuscript is putting all women on notice that we men are not going to deal with your bullshit anymore. Ladies, the scam is over. YOU WIN. This book will educate men about life skills, that they must have, to survive in the 21st century. You will learn 101 guaranteed ways to improve your marriage, and/or relationship with the beautiful lady you love.

"All Men Are Stupid", is the opinion of most American women regarding men. This is truly sad, but women in America today all think they wear the pants in a relationship and know everything. You can't tell them anything. This book teaches men and women how to be kind and respect each other from this day forward. Respect, is something that is earned, not given. Kindness, is something that is given and not earned. That being said, always treat the person you love the way you want to be respected, and everything will be just fine. Got it.

Ladies, let me set you straight, men do not beg for forgiveness. That's just plain stupid. Ladies, if you don't forgive us men for what we said, or what we did the first time we ask, then that's ok. After asking you for forgiveness and you won't accept our kindness, then we as men, don't give a shit anymore. Remember guys, we also need to forgive our ladies.

That being said, ladies, when you muck up and say something that is just plain stupid, or do something that is just plain stupid, be sure to ask your little man for forgiveness. Men forgive and forget everything you tell us in minutes, for we can't remember shit anyway. By doing this, we both know, the new communication dialogue that we are working on from this book, might even be helping.

Ladies, men already know, it's always, all about you. We hear you loud and clear. All Men Are Stupid, is the only truthful book in print about relationships where males and females are guaranteed to know what's expected from each other, to make a long term commitment work.

We have no grey areas, in this book. If these actions and understandings of these principles described in this manuscript are not acceptable to both parties, then marriage is the last thing both of you would ever want to do. A marriage at this point would just end in an expensive, painful, nasty, bitter divorce. Stop that shit today. Nobody wants that, so let's just live in sin and be friends for life. What's wrong with that?

Our behavior towards each other, is what it is, and for some reason all men and women want to do, is change each other's behavior. When you find some one that is special and beautiful on the outside, be sure he or she is right for you on the inside, too.

Remember, the only person you are guaranteed to change in your life, is yourself, don't ever forget that. If you spend your whole life trying to fix other people; you will be one, worn out, pissed off, royal pain-in-the-ass to the rest of us. Stop trying to fix everybody, it's not healthy.

This manual is a complete, truthful valuation on how you and your significant other can become better communicators. Now remember gentlemen, when your girl says she understands everything about your relationship, she really will when she has completed, "All Men Are Stupid Manuscript in its entirety". This manual contains some spelling and grammar errors, but that's ok, if you understand the basic material of this book. Women have contacted me, saying that they love our book and it has saved our marriage, but the grammar in this book is horrible. My response to them is, I hope you understand the material of this manual, for I am only here to save your relationship with the one you love. Got it. It's not about the grammar, who cares.

When I was young, I thought I knew everything about everything, from growing up in Detroit. Wow, was I wrong. This book will teach you the truth about women, marriage, families, kids, home, employment, business and sex. Women's lib my ass. Stop being nasty, you crazy bitch. The party is over. Us men get it now; we are slow to understanding women, but we got it.

Guys, you must be nice too. Ladies, men can be douche bags, jerks and assholes at times, but when we are, it's only for a short period of time. When reading the most powerful book about relationships, "All Men Are Stupid", the name calling about men and women is there to make you laugh a little and have fun with relationship learning process.

Women, in this book, are sometimes called bitches, and men are sometimes called assholes. We all know, all women are not bitches, and all men are not assholes, so relax, it's a figure of speech that will entertain you throughout this manual. Lighten up, if you don't have a sense of humor, this book might appear mighty painful. Don't take everything in so serious, enjoy life, laugh a little, and be sure to take all you have learned from this book and apply it to your life so you too can have a happy and fun relationship. That was easy.

This manual (book), is the perfect "TEST", to find out if your girl or guy, is a keeper or a throwback, just like a fish. If you have a wonderful fantastic female, and she reads this book and then pops a nasty attitude, she probable is a throwback and needs to go swimming again, and/or go play in another pond. She might be a great piece of ass, but don't marry her for Pete sake, just enjoy every bit of her until it ends, and it will end someday, you just don't know when.

If your girl reads this manual and laughs and thinks it's kind of funny, and learns some things she probable did not know about men, you may have what's called a long-term play. She may be a keeper fish and only time will tell.

Some women are still a little bit trainable, who knows, you may even have one. All ladies love to hear that. This male/female, "KEEPER TEST" that Colonel Smoke, (The Maste) has created will tell you immediately if the relationship with the one you love will last long term, or at all. This manuscript, lays the ground work for a healthy, exiting and positive relationship, as long as each person understands all the rules and expectations that have been set forth, for each other, in this book.

Colonel Smoke, " The Master" is amazing, for in All Men Are Stupid he gets your emotions all fired up, and explains how a relationship between a man and a woman is supposed to work. Some women reading this book, will get all wound up and go crazy. Let's hope that doesn't happen to yours. We will see if your partner can pass, "the keeper test"?

Some of the men reading this book needed help, for they could not understand some of the problems that their relationships were experiencing. Colonel Smoke, solves all your problems between men and women, in this book. Never again, will anything ever be confusing with your relationship once you have read, the most powerful manuscript, All Men Are Stupid in its entirety. Colonel Smoke, has laid it all out for you, so it's all crystal clear. So don't screw it all up ladies and gentlemen.

What's nice about this book, is that Colonel Smoke has designed this, male/female exclusive "KEEPER TEST", that will tell you if your fish (man or women) has any odor or bad Juju to it, kind of like taking a car for a test drive before you buy it. Who would ever buy a car without test driving it first? Answer is, nobody would be that foolish. Got to love that Colonel Smoke, (The Master) for he has figured it all out to save all your little asses. Remember gentlemen, this test works both ways and your female is always running a, "keeper test" on you too, so best for you to behave.

If your female has read our book in its entirety, she now understands men, and has read the most powerful book in the world, explaining women to men. She has learned everything you wanted her to know, that you did not have the balls to tell her yourself. Look at it this way, Colonel Smoke, (The Master) author of this fantastic book, did all the dirty work for you, and has set your woman straight on everything when it comes to men.

After reading this book, both men and women will now know all the relationship rules of life. If you choose not to comply with all these new rules, and/or adjustments that you have just learned, you are just being disrespectful to the other person and your relationship will not last long term.

Always remember, he who has the "GOLD" the money, makes all the rules. Makes sense, right. That being said ladies, if you want to make all the rules in your relationship, you need to go out and get a big paying job that makes you lots of money, and then you become the rule maker immediately. See, that was easy. Ladies, look at the education you are getting. This book will be the best information twenty dollars can buy, I promise, Colonel Smoke.

As a successful, self-employed, 51-year-old business owner, I can say today, that I only wish someone had given me a rule book like this to read. It would have saved me a lot of headaches, and hundreds of thousands of dollars throughout my lifetime. Most men today, do not have the cojones to tell their woman to shut the hell up when they say shit that is just plain stupid. Gentlemen, grow some balls, be a man, and quit acting like a girl. Men remember, sometimes it pays to listen too, you might even learn something from your girl.

Most women on the other hand, will not understand this manual, and will disagree with everything in it anyway. Once you get over the rough language, you will know, this book was written for the males and females of the world, so they can understand and improve their relationship with each the one they love. Ladies, it's never too late to learn how to be nice. Start today, you will be glad you did. Guys, we must be nice, too.

I promise, each and every one of you that reads this book, that you will become a more passionate person about life. Men, for this book to work properly, put it on the coffee table so that the magical powers of this manuscript will start working immediately. That being said, gentlemen, don't be afraid to step up and be a real man, you pussy.

This manuscript, is the advanced, higher education, counselors edition, where you will learn everything you need to know about men and women. When you complete this book, you will understand more about relationships than most counselors do. How about that? It amazing what you can learn when it's all about the truth and no bullshit.

This book, is the best gift you could ever give to a young male, and/or female that is looking to understand the opposite sex, and this book keeps on giving for life. All females need to read this book, so they can learn what's expected from them when they are in a relationship with any male. Men, be sure to tell all your friends what you have learned and make your mama proud. This book contains no BULL SHIT, and will teach you everything you need to know about men and women.

This book, was not written to bash women, but to explain to men the real truth about living with women and children over a period of 20 years. "All Men Are Stupid" – is all about teaching men to live free and enjoy every day with the DIVA they love. If you try our 101 guaranteed ways to a happy relationship, I promise you will be more satisfied with your partner and your relationship might even last long term. That was easy.

Somewhere along the way, gentlemen, we have lost our manhood with all the equal rights bullshit. Guys, you know this is true. Stop pussy footing around.

Men, only need booty and respect from their women. We are so simple. That's it. Women, make this shit so hard to understand and get so confused on everything sometimes. Women, need an emotional connection and must feel loved. Men, be sure to be kind to your women and treat her like a queen if she truly deserves it. In this world today, everyone wants to be politically correct so no one gets their feelings hurt. Fuck that shit. Real men and women, tell it like it is. It's called the truth and it can be painful. Quit trying to protect everyone's feelings. Fuck that shit. Colonel Smoke, makes everything about men and women crystal clear. By explaining everything this way, nothing any longer is confusing and/or dragged out. Enough said.

Some women reading our book, will take the book as being degrading. However, this book was not written to beat up on women, but to enlighten men on the real truths about women, and life that no one seems to have the balls to explain to men. Colonel Smoke, tells it all right here, right NOW.

Colonel Smoke, has cracked the code, and explains everything men need to know about women in this manual. We did it. So women, don't take offense to our book. Work on improving yourselves, be honest with yourselves. If you have problems, seek professional help and work on becoming a better person. Treat your man with respect if you truly love him. If not, let the poor bastard go, so as not to make him miserable for the rest of his adult life, and then you can go find your knight and shining armor and make yourself happy.

It's all about you ladies. We men, have learned this in the past few years, for sure. If for some reason your girl falls out of love with you, everything you do will be wrong in her eyes, your fucked, its life, get over it. When this happens, it is time to go shopping for a new piece of ass. You can't fix her from being nasty.

This book, was written to be serious, humorous, and entertain you throughout your journey of life to becoming a man and/or a woman. Save this book to the most popular place in your home, and refer to it often; be sure to tell all your friends, for it is the Bible if you will, for understanding each other. Never leave home without it.

It seems like no one has the *cojones* to tell the real truth about what being married, having a family, and working your ass off over the years feels like and what can go wrong. Well, I am here to tell you, that this book will open your eyes to the real facts of what life is like after high school and beyond.

Ladies, if you are upset and your blood is boiling after reading this manuscript, you have some serious problems and we need to work on them immediately. Let's get started today. The only reason you are aggravated right now with yourself, is because you are guilty of acting or behaving like the women we have described in this book. Stop being nasty today. Stop your nagging today. If the shoe fits, be sure to fess up, and wear it. Start treating your man with respect immediately, if you don't, your man will just leave and go find some new ass. That was easy.

Be sure to give your man booty and take care of all your man's needs every day, so he does not have to go elsewhere and shop at a different store. Be nice, be polite, and remember to always act like a lady, if you want to be treated like one. Guys, you need to be nice and take care of all your lady's needs, too. Don't forget to open the car door from time to time for your female, and ladies, don't forget to say, "thank you". Women, love that shit. Just had to put that in there.

The two most important things in this life to remember, and are both so hard to do; is to always forgive people that do you wrong, family is the worst. Secondly, don't rehash old shit against others for the rest of your adult life. In the big picture, does all this small petty shit that bothers you, really matter? I don't think so, it's all bull shit anyway and not healthy. All this crap does, is raise your blood pressure, and ruin a good night sleep. Let it all go. Who gives a shit? WTF.

The past is the past, and it is what it is. You can't change shit that has already happened. The only thing you can do, is move forward and improve on yourself. You can't fix stupid, so stop trying to tell other people how to do their business, and how things should be done. You need to worry about yourself only. That was easy. The END.

If you have people, and/or family, that you love but you can't stand them, stay the fuck away from them. You are not going to fix them. They are all geniuses and know everything. Always be nice to them, be kind to them, but don't get sucked into their little web of bull shit, and let them make you miserable and/or feeling guilty. Move the fuck on. Got it.

On forgiveness, if you don't learn to forgive people for doing you wrong, you will be one miserable fuck. So, if you take anything from this book, it should be to forgive everyone that has disappointed you, and move the fuck forward. It's the only way. We are only here on this planet for a blink of an eye. Don't spend all your good years trying to fix everyone and being mad at the world. It is a total waste of fucking time.

Stop and smell the flowers from time to time. Remember, if you are lucky enough to have good health, don't sweat the small shit in life, and it's all small shit if you have your health.

Now, go out and enjoy every day you are six feet above the dirt. Start today, you will be glad you did.

Ladies, being mad or upset at the author of this book, is a good thing, for at least you have realized he has touched a nerve with you, and now you understand you have some serious issues to improve on. It's never too late; you can start today and become a better person. If after reading this book, you are in agreement with our discussions, then as a woman, you should be proud of yourself for you are what every good man is looking for, and part of the one percent club. Give yourself a hand, you are a very special lady.

For the men, out there: sit back, relax, enjoy the ride, and grab a beer, for you are in for an eye-opening experience where you will now learn everything you need to know about the female brain. This has never been done like this before, and is truly amazing. Holy shit, this book, will be the best investment you can make for figuring out women and how they tick. You lucky DOG.

Remember, the younger you are, the more valuable this book will be to you financially. This manual could save you millions of dollars over your lifetime, so let's get started.

To My Mother and Father

I just want to say to my mother, "You are the best." You raised me to work hard, tell the truth, and always say my prayers. I appreciate all the things you did for me. To my father: Growing up in Detroit, Michigan, car capital of the world, was a really special time for me. I loved every bit of it. Dad, thank you for teaching me how to fly model airplanes. I look back at those days, and remember all the good times: vacationing at the Silver Lakes Sand Dunes and in Vero Beach, Florida with our family. It was an incredible journey.

To My Sister

Growing up, I did not like you too much for I always felt you got me in trouble with our father. In the end though, I have learned how intelligent and organized you are. You did a great job raising your family and I'm so proud of you.

To All My Good Friends at Our Local Café

I want to thank you for all your opinions and your accolades. If it weren't for you guys, I would not have all the right answers for my book regarding women. Love, you guys.

To All My Other Friends

Thanks to all my friends and my faith, I survived this mess with my family. I appreciate all the help with your stories and for sharing them with me. Without you, this book would not be possible.

To My Family

I also want to thank my two pain-in-the-ass children and my nasty, ungrateful ex-wife. All I can say is that, I really spoiled you guys. You were all very expensive, disrespectful, and ungrateful. I have forgiven all of you for your bad behavior and for ripping me off. It's okay; the pleasure was all mine. Lesson learned: do not spoil your family.

To My Girlfriend
You mean the world to me and you are very kind. I love you very much PK. I am truly happy you came into my life. You truly are part of the 1% of the special women on the planet. I am very proud of you.

To My Counselors
I want to thank all my counselors for ripping me off and stealing $54,645.99 with your billable hour scam. I hope you enjoyed all those fancy vacations I sent you on, and I am so glad I got to pay for them. It was so much fun; let's do it again sometime. Fuck you, you scamming counselors.

This manuscript, should be mandatory for all counselors and their patients to read. You would learn everything about life and relationships in just two hours. It is so simple. Don't make everything in your life so complicated. K.I.S.S. Keep it simple stupid.

Copyright
All rights reserved. No part of this book may be reproduced in any form or by any electronic or mechanical means, including information storage and retrieval systems—except in the case of brief quotations in articles or reviews—without the permission in writing from its publisher, Colonel B. S. Smoke.

All brand names and product names used in this book are trademarks, registered trademarks or trade names of their respective holders. I am not associated with any product or vendor in this book.

Disclaimer
This is a work of adult storytelling and is only my opinion of women and life. Names, characters, businesses, places, events and incidents are either the products of the author's imagination or used in a fictitious manner. Any resemblance to actual persons, living or dead, or actual events, is purely coincidental.

This book contains profanity and foul language. You must be over 18 years of age to read this book.

Published by COLONEL B.S. SMOKE – FIXING MARRIAGES AND RELATIONSHIPS EVERYDAY. COUNSELOR, MENTOR AND RENOWNED INTERNATIONAL SPEAKER.
COLONEL B. S. SMOKE HAS CRACKED THE CODE AND KNOWS EVERYTHING ABOUT WOMEN.

LISTEN UP BOYS AND YOU TOO CAN KNOW EVERYTHING THERE IS TO KNOW ABOUT WOMEN. IT'S ALL IN THIS ONE LITTLE BOOK, ALL MEN ARE STUPID. THIS IS THE MOST VALUABLE BOOK YOU AS A MALE OR FEMALE COULD EVER READ. GO GET THEM TIGER.

Table of Contents

Contents

Caution – All Men Are Stupid (Introduction) .**Error! Bookmark not defined.**

Table of Contents 15
Part I 19
Chapter 1   Life In A Nutshell 20
Chapter 2   Marriage Contracts Are Bad News 22
Chapter 3   It Should Cost $250K To Get Married 25
Chapter 4   The Ring Makes Me Tired 28
Chapter 5   Why Do Women Hate Sex After Having Children? 31
Chapter 6   Sex And The Counseling Scam 36
Chapter 7   Kids, Discipline, And Women 40
Chapter 8   Kids Can Be A Pain In The Ass 42
Chapter 9   Cars And Insurance With Kids 43
Chapter 10 Kids Need To Move The Hell Out When They're Eighteen 44
Chapter 11 Loins Rule: She Will Always Pick The Children Over You 46
Chapter 12 Women Always Want To Change Their Men 47
Chapter 13 Men, Women And Happiness: Can Women Ever Be Happy? 49
Chapter 14 Toys: Why Do Men Love Their Toys? 51
Chapter 15 Why Are All Women Hypersensitive? 53
Chapter 16 Blood Work Is Normal, My Ass 56
Chapter 17 Women Have To Bitch About Something All The Time 59

Chapter 18 Try Fixing Crazy Female Drama With Her Girlfriends 61
Chapter 19 Women, Stop With The Attitude 69
Chapter 20 Ladies, Stop Your Lying Today 71
Chapter 21 Women Don't Need To Know Everything 72
Chapter 22 Honey, What Are You Doing Today? 74
Chapter 23 Men Love It When You Smile 75
Chapter 24 Cheaper To Keep Her 76
Chapter 25 Internet Dating Sites Are Where It's At Today 79
Chapter 26 A Woman's Algorithm 81
Chapter 27 Women Call Them Addictions, Men Call Them Enjoyment 82
Chapter 28 Women Are Always Right 83
Chapter 29 Scorned Women Are No Good To Any Of Us Men ... 85
Chapter 30 Books, Magazines, TV, And Your Women 86
Chapter 31 Don't Spoil Your Bitch 88
Chapter 32 Women Think All Men Are Narcissistic 90
Chapter 33 Women Can Be Nasty And Greedy 93
Chapter 34 Do Women Ever Stop Drinking? 96
Chapter 35 Boob Jobs: Why Are Women Never Happy With Their Bodies? 97
Chapter 36 Jealous Women Are Nuts 98
Chapter 37 Driving A Car: Why Can't Women Use Turn Signals? 99
Chapter 38 Dream Stealing: Why Do Women Steal Our Dreams? 101

Chapter 39 Why Shopping With Women Is A Pain In The Ass 103
Chapter 40 Women Always Have To Have The Last Word ... 104
Chapter 41 Women Hold Grudges Forever 105
Chapter 42 You Have A 50/50 Shot Always To Get Booty 106
Chapter 43 Women's Questions Can Be Explosive 109
Chapter 44 Social Media And Women: 110
Chapter 45 Guys, Do Not Let Your Women Work For You ... 112
Chapter 46 Women Will Never Understand Cause And Effect 116
Chapter 47 Women Can't Understand Normal Thinking 117
Chapter 48 Why Do Girls Act Like Their Mothers? 118
Chapter 49 Child Support And Alimony 119
Chapter 50 Women And Money 121
Chapter 51 Love, Sex, And Rape 123
Chapter 52 Why All Women Should Work Outside The Home 125
Chapter 53 Life Partner? Never Thought Of That 126
Chapter 54 All Pussy Has A Price 127
Chapter 55 Men Are Tired Of Flowers And Jewelry 128
Chapter 56 Unintelligent, Stupid Conversations 129
Chapter 57 When Keeping Your Mouth Shut Will Not Work 131
Chapter 58 Prenuptial Agreements Are A Must 132
Chapter 59 Find A Girl Like Your Mother 134
Chapter 60 Quality Of Women Is Down A Little In The Twenty-First Century 136
Chapter 60.5 Women Don't Like Constructive Criticism 138

Part II Life Skills

Chapter 61 People Are A Pain In The Ass. Why? 141

Chapter 62 Forgive Everyone 142

Chapter 63 Broke People Are Lousy Advisors 144

Chapter 64 Attorneys Are All Crooks, And All Agreements Are Designed To Be Litigated 146

Chapter 65 Bankruptcy, Scams, And Cheats: Does Anybody Pay Their Bills Anymore? 149

Chapter 66 Why Is the Stock Market A Big, Money-Losing Joke? 152

Chapter 67 Insurance And Annuities Scam 155

Chapter 68 A Must Know—Rule Of 72 161

Chapter 69 Government Is A Mess: Why Does Everyone In Government Lie? 162

Chapter 70 Employment Today 163

Chapter 71 Lease Your Car: Less Stress, And Cheaper 166

Chapter 72 Home Ownership Is A Pain In The Ass: Rent vs. Own 169

Chapter 73 College Is Not For Everyone 171

Chapter 74 Parents, Get Over It: I Am Not You 172

Chapter 75 Life Insurance 173

Chapter 76 Wills Are A Must 175

Chapter 77 You May Need A Trust 176

Chapter 78 Keeping Up With The Joneses 177

Chapter 79 Be Sure to Count Your Blessings Every Day 178

Chapter 80 Animals Are Man's Best Friend 179

Chapter 81 The End 180
About the Author 191

Part I

1

Life In A Nutshell

Now, that you have purchased or was given the most powerful book in the world, "All Men Are Stupid in the eyes of the American women," you are going to learn everything you need to know about men and women, when it comes to relationships and dealing with the opposite sex. This life changing, pull know punches book, will teach you all about the challenges you are going to face in this life when it comes to relationships, and how to deal with all of life's difficult situations.

Colonel Smoke, (The Master) has created a road map, and now you too can become a relationship expert like him, and learn all the survival skills that you must have, to survive in the 21st Century. In this book, we guarantee, that we will solve all your relationship issues, once your significant other has taken the exclusive, "Keeper Test" that is included in this manuscript, free of charge. All Men Are Stupid, is the only manual on the market, that offers this exclusive TEST, and it works every time. So, let's get started. What are you waiting for?

Have you ever heard of the three F's? If it fly's, fucks or floats, rent it. Now that I have your attention, be sure to enjoy life every day. Lease your car, rent a house, get snipped (a vasectomy), get two dogs to love on you, become a boyfriend or girlfriend to a nice person, and enjoy every day you are six feet above the dirt. Got it. That was easy.

Your parents and grandparents will disagree and won't understand most of the shit in this book, for they grew up in a different era. Trust me when I say, "old folks do not understand today's world, and they don't want to". All good things must come to an end, it's called life.

Now, that you have heard of the 3 F's, let me tell you about the four F's. Faith, Family, Friends and Fun? Faith, don't let anyone steal your faith in your God, for it is the most powerful belief on earth. Family, can be a pain in the ass, but always be respectful to them. Some family members are going to be nasty and disrespectful, just be kind to them, and let them go. Don't try to fix everyone in your family, you can't. Friends, only be friends with people that bring positive and kindness to your heart. All Debbie downers, from this point forward, must find other friends, you quit. Fun, always make sure that what you do long-term, brings excitement and fun into your life. Your job needs to be something you enjoy, or you need to go find another job. Life is exciting and fun if you work in something that brings joy into your heart. Remember, with the four F's, it's all about you becoming a better person.

Be sure to be positive every day, and make the best of everything, and you will have a fulfilling life with peace, love, and happiness. This book, contains some foul language, but get over it; its life and we are not going to hell for it. Got it.

This manuscript, will help your lady understand how to make herself a better person to the man she loves. All women reading this book, will now understand the fundamentals of what it takes to make their man happy, and will now know how to be supportive of his needs. Men, will learn to be a little more compassionate and understanding with their female they love. It's all part of All Men Are Stupid.

This is the "ONLY" tell all book, with the free, exclusive, "KEEPER TEST" available for men and women on the market. Ladies, listen up, you might even learn something here. Guys, you need to listen too, it's only fair.

2

Marriage Contracts Are Bad News

Marriage, is the real deal. Marriage contracts are great – if you live in America, plan to make no money, and stay broke for the rest of your adult life. If you are young and have no plans to make big money, or win the lottery, then getting married is for you. When you have no assets to split and have no money, it's easy to get divorced, and/or become separated. 0 minus 0 is always 0.

The most important thing you need to remember is, THIS BOOK IS A MUST READ BEFORE MARRIAGE, for after you get married, you have zero leverage over anything in this book that you have learned. You are fucked. So, if you are smart ladies and gentlemen, you will read this book from cover to cover, immediately. The End.

The leverage created with a marriage contract in America is a legal scam, that will fuck you forever, when getting divorced. The attorneys, forensic auditors, mediators, accountants, investigators, book keepers, researchers, attorney assistants, assistants to the attorney's assistant, tax lawyers, behavior counselors, counselor's counselors', therapist of all fucking sorts, and professionals that you have never even heard of, will fuck you so hard when getting divorced, that you can't see straight. This shit is not funny. This is the biggest fucking scam going in America today, and no one seems to want to talk about it, but I, Colonel Smoke, tell it all.

These scamming, pieces of shit attorney's, cost hundreds of thousands of dollars. This scam never stops once you start. Remember, your wonderful prenuptial agreement that you signed before marriage to save your ass, gets litigated too. It's all part of our fantastic, fucked-up legal system, here in America. Shoot them all.

A PRENUPTIAL AGREEMENT IS A MUST. DO NOT GET MARRIED WTHOUT A SIGNED, NOTORISED AND WITNESSED PRENUPTIAL AGREEMENMT. Getting married without a prenuptial agreement is like committing financial suicide. It's like jumping out of a perfectly good airplane without a parachute, now that is just fucking stupid.

Most of this shit about having a prenup makes no sense to you when you are in love with the one and only, but wait to the shit hits the fan, and it will hit the fan, someday, you just don't know when, trust me. The problem is, when you fuckers fall in love and get all fucked up, you can't see straight. You are thinking with the wrong head, you dumb ass. My job, as the author of this book, is to wake you the fuck up and get your head out of your ass. If he or she won't sign the prenup, then don't get fucking married, you asshole. That was easy. THE END.

Now remember, if you were lucky enough to have married some rich bitch, and she pays all your bills, then shut the fuck up and be happy, you dick. If the marriage doesn't work out, then just take half of what she's got and move the fuck on. That was easy. It's always nice when somebody else has to pay for all the legal bills. I kind of like that.

These wonderful attorneys, "pieces of shit" work only to steal all your assets and your money. Once your money is all gone, they quit scamming you and go the fuck away, and then they must find somebody else to fuck with. Just shoot all these assholes. They bring absolutely nothing to this society, but their scamming, evil ways. Attorneys quit fucking you, when they are dead, imagine that.

If you plan to make real money, plan for retirement or receive a pension, marriage in America is a big bad joke. You're fucked. DO NOT DO IT. THE END. Ladies, don't forget if you are of means (rich), you don't need a guy to fuck up your shit either. Rent your guy, and everything will be just fine. It works both ways. That was easy.

3

It Should Cost $250K To Get Married

Take the $250,000 marriage test: sign over all the assets that you have acquired through today—cars, money, planes, toys, and cash pensions—to your significant other, and then sign a promissory note to pay that bitch $5,000 every month, for the next three years. If, after paying her $5,000 per month for three years and giving her everything you own, you still love this scenario, you deserve to be married to that bitch.

This is what divorce looks like when your marriage ends and you get fucked for the rest of your adult life, until death. *Wow—no one ever told me that.* Ha! That's why this book is a must-read for both men and women.

A law should be imposed: if you want to get married, you pay $250,000 to the state you reside in, as a marriage license fee. With this new law, a divorce in your state would be free and no attorneys would be needed to fuck you.

Scamming attorneys and their experts are expensive. With this law, you will not get fucked by our legal system, for you will not need any of these assholes to get divorced. By initiating this new law, you will eliminate 98% of the aggravation of getting married. No one has $250,000 to invest to do something so stupid. Fuck that shit.

Marriage, could be the worst financial decision you will ever make in your adult life, if you ever have to get divorced. The problem is that it costs $5 to get married, and millions to get divorced. Don't get married unless you plan on being broke for the rest of your adult life. Rent it all. That shit was easy. Problem solved. Now remember, if your bitch has 20 million in the bank, marry her today. This is a little confusing to you, I know, but money talks.

In today's world, 60% (estimated) of marriages end up in divorce. The other 39% (estimated) of you fuckers, just live in misery till the day you die. And 1% (estimated) of you fucks live with peace, harmony, and joy with your lovely and wonderful lady. That's nice. Fuck you. As a friend of mine once said, it's cheaper to keep the bitch, and just have a hooker when I need booty if she is not going to give it up. Okay, that works too. Whatever works for you, just make yourself happy, for life is short, and you are only here on the planet for a blink of an eye.

Marriage should be like a car lease; you take the marriage contract for a period of three years at a time (36 months). This way if your wife gets a bad motor, her brain shorts out, or she just gets a case of the nasties, you just trade her in for a newer, sexier model, and don't renew the lease. If she still treats you right and drives good, then renew her for an additional three years (36 months).

Now, that makes common fucking sense, and makes life so much easier. By doing it this way, everyone knows that they could be replaced by a new model. In today's world, you only keep your car for as, long as it treats you good. The day its starts wearing out or acting up, it's got to go. What's wrong with that? Just be nice, you crazy bitch. Guys, that goes for you too, asshole.

The best advice I can give you when it comes to your sanity and dealing with your bitch, is to just keep your mouth shut when it comes to stupid conversations about marriage.

Trying to reason with today's women, (who all know everything anyway), is like playing with skunks. You will get sprayed and you will lose. The moral of the story, is to keep your fucking mouth shut at all times—you will never win any battles with your bitch if you open your mouth. That was easy. Are you learning anything here?   This shit is so simple, shut the fuck up, you asshole. Got it.

As you can see, the money you spent for this book, has already paid for itself on the first two chapters, and you will save hundreds of thousands of dollars over a lifetime if you follow all of our instructions. We are just getting started! By the time you finish this book, you will know everything there is to know about men and women.   Now, keep reading you dumb ass.

4

The Ring Makes Me Tired

Every woman wants a ring on their finger so that she can start controlling her little man. Fuck that shit. The ring, in my opinion, is the death wish to your freedom and fun. Once you're married, you lose all the leverage in the relationship. You become a puppet on a string. You get to do whatever that bitch wants you to do. You get to pay for whatever she wants, and you are now her meal ticket for life. That kind of sucks.

Now, you must listen to all the stupid shit about her girlfriends, their fantastic husbands, their wonderful kids, their exciting vacations, etc., while your girl says she has nothing. Remember, you get to pay for everything now, and when you get divorced, you still get to pay for everything. What the fuck is that all about? Now that's fucked up.

Can you imagine signing yourself up for no sex, no blowjobs, and no kinky sex under the stars? Its prison, guys. Don't do it. Actually, prison is easier than some marriages. If you learn anything from this book, it's that if you are single today, you are one blessed guy. Don't fuck up your life from here on out. This book was written because your little head does the thinking for your big head, and then you are in the life of hell till death do you part. Do you understand?

Marriage in the old days worked. Sorry boys, but the world has changed. Today in America, it is a leverage tool to get fucked over by the opposite sex, for the rest of your adult life. Would you like to know what I really think? Now remember, 1% of you fucktards are living a happy, joyous, wonderful life with the person you love, we got it.

Most people have no clue, that marriage is a contract between two parties that can only be broken, and/or terminated by the courts, and/or death. Marriage contracts create leverage for bad behavior in women, so that they can become nasty and ugly, and this is where it gets expensive to fix. That being said, in America, most legal issues are paid for by the male, so for that reason, be careful about signing contracts, for they can become very expensive. Remember, all marriage contracts and divorce litigation are terminated on death.

Women, don't seem to understand money and time either. If it's my money and my time being used for something, it's probable going to be my way. This is not narcissism, but it is common sense. Now, if you have a rich bitch, and you are on her dime, and on her time, let it be her way. This is sometimes difficult for women to understand completely. Ladies, you are more than welcome to pay for everything, with your big job, if you want things to be done your way. Men have no problems with this, for you females all know everything anyway.

Most marriages end in divorce, and the divorce is never fair. The two guarantees in life are death and taxes. That's it. Happiness and fairness are not guarantees. I hope I have helped you so that you do not make the same mistakes I did. At 18 years of age, you are one cocky little fucker and think you know everything. After getting goat-fucked by a woman, you lose all your zest for life. Don't do it. Live life every day to the fullest and be grateful you're alive. It's a fantastic life, if you don't fuck it all up. Rent.

So, next time she brings up the ring thing, ask your bitch if your laundry is done and folded yet? By diverting and changing the subject (now that we know that scam, gentlemen), you can possibly get out of the marriage conversation and talk about something else, like the weather or something.

Your woman may not want to get married when she learns that in some countries, married women are called, *registered man servants*. The Bahamas does it this way. I love the Bahamas. I don't believe the title, *"registered man servant"* is exactly what a woman is looking for when she is getting married. I wonder who thought of this fantastic idea, its genius.

If for some reason you are lucky enough to meet some bitch who has $20 million in the bank—verified, certified, notarized, and witnessed—and she weighs less than 369 pounds, our guy's rule book says, "marry that bitch today". Give her a ring, love on her, and marry her. When she gets tired of your shit, take half of everything she has and be fucking happy. So yes, ladies, if you are rich enough and put out, we will put a ring on it and marry your ass until death do us part. Gentlemen, this is called find a rich bitch (Sugar Momma) and marry her ass. That was easy. What's next?

In the Bible, it says somewhere, that God took a rib from Adam and created Eve, so that man would not be alone. Being alone is not the way God intended for us to live. There is somebody out there for everyone, and in life you should never give up trying to find your soul mate. Once you find your true partner, always be grateful, kind, and appreciative for someday they will be gone, too. Women, should always take care of their man and men should always worship the ground their woman walks on. All this is so very easy, if everyone would just follow our simple directions.

5

Why Do Women Hate Sex After Having Children?

Everyone is excited when you bring a new baby into this world. Your family and friends are overjoyed, and the happiness is abundant. Raising kids is a big job. When they are newborns, they need food, water, diaper changes, rocking, it's endless. Little kids are cute. Enjoy it while it lasts. The first few years are fun; watching them crawl and take their first steps is exciting. Just remember, today those little fuck sticks will cost you $1 million apiece (estimated), over your lifetime. Now, do they really bring that much joy? I don't think so. No way.

A vasectomy, costs about $350 (estimated), and you pay cash for it only once. It's extra insurance to avoid unwanted children. Sometimes your lady will conveniently forget to take her birth control and the next thing you know, gentlemen, you have another million-dollar liability. Ain't that just great? You ask yourself, how did that shit happen? Remember guys: you get to pay for your child emotionally, physically, financially and mentally for the rest of your adult life. Now, that's fucking wonderful. Get a dog, you asshole, their easy.

Having a baby is supposed to be a fun time. I call bullshit on this one! If your girl gets postpartum depression, which is very common for women today, it will be everything *but* fun. Postpartum depression is a very serious matter.

Postpartum depression, is moderate to severe depression in a woman after she has given birth. It may occur soon after delivery or up to a year later. Most of the time, it occurs within the first three months after delivery. When your female delivers this beautiful baby and then goes straight into depression, because her hormones are all screwed up due to the pregnancy, you're screwed. Remember, you are so low on the totem pole, your girl can't even remember your name. Go figure.

A women's entire physical and mental body makeup has changed. She's overweight, her old clothes do not fit, and she can be very mean and nasty. Guys, if this happens to you, you must get your girl professional help immediately, and say your prayers. The bullshit never stops. Guys, go walk your dog and hope your girl snaps out of it, or you will have one more thing to deal with for the rest of your adult life. Holly fuck. I can't take this shit anymore.

At five years of age, kids go to kindergarten and make some new friends, and the parents get a little time to enjoy their small amounts of freedom when their children are not around. The father thinks he might get some booty now that the children are gone during the day, but the wife forgets all about her man's needs on purpose, and only makes time for shopping, girlfriends, and/or coffee by herself. You, on the other hand, are just a pain in her ass. Children, because they came from her loins will always take precedence over you. Once a woman has one or two babies, you are just a breadwinner to support the financial kingdom that you started. Stop that shit immediately, you asshole.

Sex? What the hell is that after a woman has delivered babies? She never wants to see that little penis ever again. When women have kids, your sex life is over and the fun train stops. I think that women, once they deliver children into this world and have experienced the birthing process, wants nothing to do with sex. All of a sudden, when you want a piece of ass, they're tired, they have a headache, they're on their period, the kids will hear, or the garbage man will know. Who the fuck cares?

When you're married (committed), it's like you have to beg for booty. Remember, when you were just dating, getting a piece of ass was easy. That shit stops on marriage. If you never want to get pussy again, get married, and I promise you it will STOP. It's only a matter of time, you just don't know when. It's guaranteed to stop, and you have no control over it. That's just fucking great. If you're only renting it, and not married to it when it cuts you off, you can move out the old and find some new. That was easy. Women make this shit so complicated.

Women, think that when they cut you off from getting booty, you are no longer getting laid. Women, I am here to inform you, you're wrong. Guys, just go elsewhere once they have to beg for pussy. If you're married, this is called adultery. When renting it, it's called a hookup. Whatever it's called, you need to explain to your bitch, that you are going to get booty one way or another until death. You would prefer to tap her ass, but if she cuts herself off from you, (her decision), then she has just given you permission to go tap some new ass. It's not complicated. That should be written somewhere inside the marriage license. Now that makes common sense.

All guys want from life is respect from their girl and getting laid three times a week. That's it. Women, make this shit so complicated. It's NOT. Men can't figure out why women don't understand this concept. It's fucking simple: Put out or get out, bitch. Don't over complicate it. Do you understand? That was easy. Rent it.

All men go to strip clubs and it's a natural thing. Ladies, do not get pissed off, or cut your man off if he occasionally stops in at a strip club for a beer with friends, and looks at all the pretty ass that is there. The stresses of home life, kids, and employment wear him out and he just wants to dream and relax a little. There is nothing wrong with this behavior; he is a man. He does not fuck every woman in the strip club like you think. Okay, enough said.

Now that we've got that handled, take care of your man and give him a personal show in the bedroom occasionally, to keep him interested and excited about you. Men are not that hard to understand; we are very simple-minded. Booty and respect is all we need. You ladies get so confused sometimes. Do you understand now? You might forget to do the laundry, walk the dog, and/or do the dishes, but don't ever forget to take care of all your man's needs, for if you do forget, he will just have to make other plans. That was easy.

Men, work hard, play hard, enjoy a cold beer every once-in-a while, and we need booty. Women, if you're reading this book, take care of your man's needs properly and I promise you that he will be faithful and worship the ground you walk on. Blowjobs are a must, for you to keep your man. Got it.

When you are first dating, you get blowjobs freely—in your office, in your car, and at home. But once the relationship is considered "long-term" or you get married, all this shit stops. What's up with that? Ladies, do you have a problem with this? Are you changing the rules of the game again? Holy Shit. What the fuck is up with you, now? You ladies, make all of us men tired and confused. We can't figure you ladies out!

Women, need to respect their men and always be nice. They need to learn to treat they're man the way they treat their kids, their friends, and their dogs. I will never forget my friend's father-in-law, who used to get rotten bananas and apples in his lunch pail that his wife prepared for him. I asked him one time, what the hell that was all about, and he said his wife gives him all the rotten leftover crap to eat. She always treated him like shit, so he just went along with it for the kids' sake, and kept a girlfriend on the side just to keep the family together. Problem solved, that was easy.

Guys, this is not the way to live. Fuck that shit, throw that bitch out. That will teach her. They will eventually learn to be nice and take care of their man, or they must get the fuck out. Some women are slower than others to figure this shit out.

Don't ever let yourself be disrespected by some bitch who thinks her pussy is golden. That shit is a dime a dozen and the next train is right around the corner. Never commit to a scorned, fucked-up woman. Once they are scorned, they are no longer good for any one of us. Rent it. Got it?

Are you learning something here? I think so. This manual, will be the most valuable manuscript you will ever read, and will teach you everything you ever needed to know about women and men. Women, can be beautiful if they want too. It's never too late to start. Men, on the other hand, if treated with respect can be very kind, also. So, ladies and gentlemen, get your shit together and don't forget, you are all taking the "Keeper Test" right the fuck, now. Some of you, when you get done with this book, are no longer going to be together. Others, are going to realize, that you are meant for one another. Which one our you?

6

Sex And The Counseling Scam

Sex, is a must. Ladies, be sure to take care of your man. Good old hard-core sex, is a must to keep your man satisfied. This means ladies, that you have to have sex throughout all your hormonal escapades, and beyond for life; this is not a part-time job, bitch.

That being said, if a woman decides to cut off the pussy from her man, because of a headache, she is tired, she is not in a good mood, etc., a guy should just get a free pass, for a strange piece of ass without the female getting all upset. But instead you have to go to counseling for the rest of your adult life. That's fucked up. Ladies, are you starting to understand how it's supposed to work yet? Get your shit together, please, or get the fuck out. The End.

Men, the rules are that you should always start in your own backyard, (your girl), but if you get turned down for sex for whatever reason, then just go next door and grab the next train. Remember guys, we never beg for sex. That's just plain stupid. So ladies, next time you cut your man off, understand that you have given him a free pass, to tap any ass, since you have closed your store. Ladies, you cannot shop at a closed store, you already know that. Always leave your store open, if you want your man to shop only in your store. Men are good with commitment, until the first time her store is closed and cuts off the pussy. After that, we don't care.

When was the last time a man turned down a female? Never, it's not going to happen, LADIES. Your bitch needs to shit or get off the pot. The days of women being nasty, and controlling when they won't give you any pussy, are over.

Now, that we got this all straightened out, be sure to explain the new rules to your lady, so that she does not get the whole thing fucked up and drag your ass into counseling. Counseling, is another fucked up scam that men need to know about. If you ever decide to go to counseling for help to fix your relationship with your bitch, most of the time you will find that counselors will always blame the male individual in the relationship, even though you're not the whole problem. Here is how this scam works: counselors work on the same billable hour scam that attorneys do.

When the professional counselor gets a new client, they figure out how much money you have, so they can bill as many billable hours as they can, to keep the client on the books for as long as they can. This way, they can steal all the cash, and/or credit card access that you have. This is why the counselor ask all those questions about what you do for employment and how many long hours do you work? If you are unemployed, and have no money, you don't have any problems that require counseling. Counselors, don't care about you, if you are broke. You are just fucking broke. Holy fuck, go solve all your own problems, you asshole.

It's never about helping the client and fixing the real problem; it's all about the counselor padding his or her pockets with billable hours, so that they can go on an extended vacation with your money. I love paying for somebody else's vacation. Fuck that shit, I am done. The game is fucking over. The reason counselors pick on the male and tell us we're all fucked up, is because they know we will just blow it all off, and keep paying them since our bitch tells us, too.

If a professional counselor, tells a woman she has issues and needs to work on some areas to improve herself, the woman will just stop going to counseling, and the billable hour scam will end abruptly for the professional counselor. Remember guys, you are always the one fucked up. It such bull shit, fuck counseling, It's a scam. You can learn more from this book, than any counselor could ever think of teaching you. Every professional doctor, lawyer, broker, and counselor, etc. wants to get on board and help you solve all your personal problems, so that they can then become part of your payment plan and steal all your money. When you run out of cash, somehow you're miraculously cured of all your problems. It's amazing how this shit works.

When getting counseling, the counselor always wants individual sessions. First they want you, then your partner, then they want the individual children, then they want your neighbor, then they want your parents, then they want the neighbor's dog, then they want any combination of all the above together, and/or separately. This is a fucking joke.

Second, they all use the same techniques in their practices, including behavioral therapy, cognitive behavioral therapy, family system therapy, psychodynamic therapy, mindfulness training therapy, shock therapy. What the fuck is all this shit you ask? Fuck, the professional counselor, does not even know what this shit means, but I guarantee, it's expensive. You should ask the professional counselor, to spell half of this shit. Are you fucking kidding me? No wonder why the bill never stops? What the fuck?

Guys, this billable scam shit is expensive. I spent well over $50,000 on this shit, and my family is more fucked up than ever. Don't do it. It's a waste of money and time. Instead of therapy, let's try this, men stop being an asshole and ladies quit being a nasty, miserable bitch. Problem solved. The End.

Counselors, also talk slowly and rephrase every sentence, so no one's feelings get hurt. They always change the tone to confuse the shit out of everybody so that they can continue their billable hour scam. Fuck counseling. It's just another professional scam, that women love to do so that they can get someone to listen to all their fucked-up problems. A counselor pretends to care, and they love to listen to your woman's shit, for as many hours as you can afford to pay. If you pay my ass $200 per hour, I will sit and listen to your females fucked up issues and pretend to care, too. It's all a scam. Counseling, should take 10 minutes to solve any problem that your bitch may have. By reducing the time, the billable hour scam, does not work well for the professional counselors.

Guys, if you get sucked into this bullshit, just tell the counselor that we now know the billable hour scam, and that we have decided that the counselor has one hour to fix all our family problems, and then we're fucking done. That's it. At this point, thank the counselor nicely for his or her time, and tell them to have a fantastic day, and enjoy all the money that he or she stole from you. Remember gentlemen, you can't fix stupid and/or stupid behavior, if no one is accountable for their actions, and just wants to blame others, nothing will work.

Ladies, always remember, to take your hormonal medication before counseling; counseling will not work if your hormones are all out of whack. The moral of the story here ladies, if you cut your man off from pussy, he will just go next door to the first available, next in line, just like a restaurant. That was easy. Men are all done with the counseling scam. Ladies, we now know the game. It's over. Do you think you understand? Have I said enough, yet? Fuck all that bullshit. Ladies and gentlemen, you want to make your relationship work, just start being respectful and kind to each other, every day. Problem solved, that was easy.

7

Kids, Discipline And Women

Today's American children are; lazy, disrespectful, and are the most ungrateful fucks to their parents, teachers, and employers. These ungrateful little shits, you can't spank, and/or discipline, or you will go to jail. Children today, know everything and are all geniuses because of the Internet. Right or wrong, the Internet is giving your children good and bad information about life every day.

Raising children in America, is a big pain in the ass. In a 24-hour day, kids sleep for 12 hours during the day and party all night long. Some go to school, some don't. WTF. They have fun with their friends all day. They won't call you back. They won't tell you where they are, and they won't even show up for dinner. What the fuck is up with that?

How are you supposed to raise good kids, if you only have 30 minutes a day with them, and they spend that time arguing about everything with you? Fifty percent of these little shits don't even graduate. Today's children, wear pants down to their knees, they slouch, they have attitudes, and they slur all their fucked-up words, so you can't even understand what the fuck they are saying. Don't spoil these little bastards, or they will never leave home. Get them the fuck out today. You will be glad you did. I give up.

By now, you probably know that the author of this book, has raised two royal pain-in-the-ass children, that were very expensive, and did not bring that much joy into his life. He loves both of his children deeply, but their behavior, is atrocious. Some of you will have perfect children, and I am truly happy for you. All children are cut from a different cloth, and I am here to tell you that some of you will be very lucky and are blessed, for you have wonderful kids. This is fantastic.

The rest of us struggle every day trying to reason with our children's crazy behavior, drug addictions, alcohol addictions, thievery, financial problems, and crazy drama. Pray for us folks, for it has not been easy, and we as parents are doing the best job we can with the bundles of joy we were given, enough said. It's a lot of work. Wrap that rascal, you will be glad you did.

8

Kids Can Be A Pain In The Ass

As kids get older, my advice would be not to spoil them. Children, have many wants and will not stop whining until they get what they want. If you give in, you will have the most disrespectful, and ungrateful bastards on the planet. Don't do it. All children must earn everything. At first, this sounds harsh, but once you have spoiled the little brats, your life is hell until death.

Chores, are a great way for children to learn value. They could be cleaning their rooms, mowing the grass, or washing the car. If you pay your children to complete their chores, then the value of a dollar is determined. I did all this wrong. I just spoiled mine, and have two disrespectful, expensive and ungrateful children. The more you give, the more they want. Don't spoil those little bastards.

Children, must earn the right to have cell phones. If you give your child a cell phone that has not been earned by hard work, he or she will lose it, break it, or will not respect it. If your child insists that he or she needs a phone, never deny them. Just explain to them that they can get one, at their own expense whenever they want. Parents, owe their children nothing, but food and shelter. That's all. Don't go crazy trying to please these little pain-in -the-asses all the time, for it will drive you BONKERS, and you never will be good enough for them anyway. You are just a shitty parent, so get over it, life goes on. That's ok

9

Cars And Insurance With Kids

I learned a valuable lesson here, too. All vehicles, must be paid for by the wanna-be-adult-child, who knows everything and thinks he or she is a genius. The child must have a job working part-time to pay for the vehicle and insurance is a must. I paid for my children's insurance, and my daughter wrecked the car and did not care. The premium went up after the claim, and she still did not care. This is bull shit.

Make them pay and have their own car insurance, that way when they wreck the car, it's not your problem. It's theirs. THE END. Problem solved.

Cars, are like cell phones: children need to earn them. This way, they will respect and value them. Teach your children to check the fluid, tires, and be sure they know cars need quarterly service. Remember, if they are paying for their own car, they will take care of it. If not, they will wreck, trash, and destroy it. Remind them, walking and riding a bike works, too.

Most of these wonderful, fantastic children are smart enough not to destroy or wreck, what they themselves pay for. That's called common fucking sense. Hopefully your kids are smart enough to not wreck shit that they have paid for. Enough about cars!

10

Kids Need To Move The Hell Out When They're Eighteen

If you are a parent, the best advice I can give you is this: as soon as Johnny or Susie is 18 years of age and graduates high school, he or she needs to move the hell out of your home, immediately. This way, the nonsense stops. Let these fucksticks experience the world their own way, because they know everything anyway, and all you're going to do is piss them off. Remember, all children that are a royal pain- in- the -ass are called fucksticks, if they are under the age of 20. After the age of 20, they are all geniuses, and know everything, yet they can't make enough money to move the hell out, and/or support themselves. These children are called fucktards. I know this sounds rough, but wait to your child gets in their teenage years, and then you will understand. Until then, it's a cake walk. When your child starts to drive is when it all goes to hell. Good luck.

I, as a parent, don't understand how kids can know everything about everything, and yet they can't keep a job, and/or show up for school. What the hell! Whatever you decide to call your children, they are still a royal pain- in- the -ass. Remind these wonderful children, that once the move out, they can smoke pot, they can get drunk, they don't have to make their beds, and we no longer care if they party and stay out all night. As soon as they leave the house, you will be the happiest son of a bitch around. The arguing, and all of the nonsense stops when they move out. That was easy. Remember, some children never leave the nest because you have spoiled them. Throw them out today. It's the only way. THE END.

Remember though, when the kids move out, your woman will go right into depression. Now, that these little fucksticks are gone, your girl can't get out of bed, for she is not caring for them anymore. She worries and thinks about them 24-7. Now listen up: take her to the doctor, and get her some depression medicine so that she can function. Remember, your job as a guy is never done until death. You must listen to all your family's stupid shit, and fix and pay for all their fucked-up problems, until you die. Now, that just fantastic. Once your children are gone, you would think you might start getting laid again. Not going to happen. Your girl, will worry about those fuck sticks, that she no longer has to mother, and she will barely be able to function, because of all the anxiety and/or depression. WTF.

Holy shit—it never ends. This is why men have a midlife crisis and need girlfriends, cars, boats, planes and trains: just to survive and keep their sanity. Do not ever let your children move back into your homestead after they have moved out to go to college, and/or work. They have learned so many unhealthy behavioral habits living outside of your home, that you will fight with them 24-7 trying to renegotiate all the crap you already tried to teach them when they were growing up in your home. They will not respect the rules of the house, and they will disobey every one of them. It's not worth it; do not do it. Do not collect your 200.00 dollars. Do you understand?

Get them out of the house. Only give them the first month's rent, and a security deposit for a new apartment. That was easy. Remember, we never cosign a lease or sign a promissory note for our children; it will burn you every time. Raising a family in today's society is a big pain- in- the- ass. As you can see, it's expensive as hell, it's exhausting, and the bullshit never stops. This is why I suggest getting snipped (a vasectomy), at 18 years of age, getting two dogs, and renting everything else. It's easier. Got it? Now, we have solved all your problems with children, your life will be fantastic.

11

Loins Rule: She Will Always Pick The Children Over You

It never made sense to me, but a woman, will always rule in favor of her kids, instead of their man. Children today, can be the biggest pains in the ass. They are disrespectful, lazy, and ungrateful, yet the woman always sides with the children. As you now know, you can't spank your children, or discipline them, or you'll go to jail. What the hell?

Children, have more rights than you do as an adult. If you have pain-in-the-ass children, your girlfriend or your wife will always side with the kids. If you ever get into an altercation with your woman, where she must choose sides between her kids or you, her kids will always win out. She did not carry you for nine months or birth you into the world, so you will never have the true power of pregnancy on your side. You may have participated by fertilizing the egg with an X or a Y chromosome, but to your woman that doesn't mean shit. You are just a piece of shit, go back to work, you asshole. Got it.

Never get between her and her kids, because you will always lose. In life, you are learning that nothing is fair, and that you as a man have to listen to all that bullshit from emotional women, and fucked up children. This is why men die earlier than women. The shit gets so deep, it smothers us. Be sure you have a big shovel to keep above it all. Good fucking luck, you will need it.

12

Women Always Want To Change Their Men

Women, are never happy just leaving their man alone. When you meet a nice girl, you get to know her, you are impressed with her, and you pray that she will stay nice like this, her whole entire life. Good luck. When women meet men, they look into their eyes, and think of all of your good qualities and how they can mold each man to make him better for *themselves*. This is called "being in women's Lifetime Boot Camp 101." Do not do it. It's very dangerous.

In reality, guys are fine the way they are, and just want to be left the fuck alone. Ladies, why is it so hard for you to comprehend this shit? Stop trying to always change your man. Women, on the other hand, change like the direction of the wind. They get messed up from their girlfriends, their religious beliefs, their parents, their coworkers, PMS, postpartum depression, menopause, chemical imbalances, and every other damn thing. What the fuck is up with that, it never stops!

The person you choose to marry, is not the same person you will divorce. By then, she has turned into a crazy, nasty, miserable bitch. Most women, will become scorned over time, can't move on, and must hold a grudge forever against their man. Women, never forget anything, you do, that they don't like, but they always forget all the good things that you do for them every day. That's fucked up.

Men, on the other hand, are so busy working, repairing the homestead, and fixing the cars that they can't remember shit and hold no grudges. Women are constantly changing. You never know day to day, if your girl is on the rag, menopausal, or depressed until she wakes up and says, good morning. You on the other hand, get up and are just happy to be six feet above the dirt. Go figure. What the fuck is up with that?

Guys, all I can say is that women are complicated, and they have plumbing that is guaranteed to break somewhere and fail. Plug all the holes that you can, and enjoy the best ride that you can. Life is short. Don't be miserable, and don't let that bitch make you miserable. The next nasty bitch you deal with must get the fuck out immediately. Got it? That was easy. I don't do nasty or crazy anymore. I am done. The End.

All women want to do is nest, mold their little man, and get married. This is a financial trap and nothing good can come from it. Once you're trapped in this crazy behavior, you will get killed. It's fucking expensive; rent it, instead. When you are renting it, you are paying for it to leave, says Charlie Sheen. It is so much easier. Got it? Guys, is this starting to make sense? Are you learning something here?

A man's dream every day, is to wake up, and have a cup coffee, go to work, make a little money for his family, have a nice dinner when he gets home, and tap a piece of ass before he retires to bed, all without his female bitching about something he did, or did not do. That's a man's dream, pretty simple but yet, some women, make this shit so fucking complicated. WTF.

LADIES, YOU MUST TAKE CARE OF YOUR MAN BEFORE YOU TAKE CARE OF THE KIDS, THE DOG, YOUR JOB, YOUR HOUSE, ETC. Do you think you can do that? It's not that hard bitch, get your priorities right, please. Thank you for your cooperation in advance. Remember ladies, todays man, will just leave if you can't get it right.

13

Men, Women And Happiness: Can Women Ever Be Happy?

Women, can only stay happy for three days, max. Women, always have to get their way, or their not happy. I don't understand this, but it is true. Women worry about every damn thing that does not concern them, and is not their direct problem. That being said, women, try to fix everything at work, in their families and with all their fucked-up girlfriends. Guys, we have all dealt with their fucked-up girlfriends. "When your bitch is not happy, you're not going to be happy". This is a cliché, that is true in today's world. Women, have to tell us about all this shit that does not matter to us at all. They have to get involved in everyone else's business. It's just their fucking nature, I guess.

When you start dating your little man, everything is good. You love on him, the sex is great, you together, party like it is 1969, but after a while things change. You might have had a couple of kids, your bills are out of control, and your man is no longer giving you the attention you want or need. He is a piece of shit. The new you, gets mad about everything that used to make you happy, and now you have changed into a miserable, crazy bitch. The world is all wrong and you start blaming everything that does not go your way, on your little man. WTF.

This hatred and or resentment for your man, is not good. The moral of the story here ladies is, if you ever get where you can't stand being around your man, or you hate him so much that you are just plain miserable; you have to decide to either get happy and/or take your medicine or let your little man go.

Men, are all done putting up with today's nasty women, that are all full of hate and resentment. This behavior, is totally unacceptable and we will not kiss your ass anymore. We will just move the fuck out and go find some new ass. This is where, Colonel Smoke, (The Master) says, if your hormones are out of control, and/or your thyroid has quit working, be sure to seek a medical doctor immediately that understands hormone replacement therapy, and be sure to take your fucking medicine. That was easy. Guys, same for you, if you have a hate problem towards your girl and you are always miserable when you are around her, be sure to seek medical help so as not to ruin everything you have both worked for. Sometimes, relationships just end, they just do. Its life.

In closing, hatred is a terrible thing. Be sure to relax, chill, and have fun every day, and remember if you hate someone to the point where you are miserable and can't take it anymore, get the fuck away from them. Some people are just not made to be together, It's that simple. Stop going back into the fire. One has to live life to the fullest every day, and be happy for one day it all comes to an end anyway. GET HAPPY TODAY, you will be glad you did.

Guys, are happy by just going fishing, watching football, going to a strip club, or going to the track, etc. For us, happiness is just getting away from our fucked-up families and friends, and doing any of the above. Women, as I said, have a three-day maximum happy time before they must bitch about something you did, did not do, or should have done. Remember, when you're married to an unhappy woman, you are fucked for life, until death. When you rent an unhappy woman, you are stuck until her shit is out of your home. Don't make yourself miserable trying to please some bitch that is always nasty. You can never make her happy, if she is always going to be miserable. Life is too short to put up with her always being unhappy. That was easy, rent that shit. Got it.

14

Toys: Why Do Men Love Their Toys?

God giveth; women taketh away. Have you ever heard of this before? It's true, gentlemen. All toys are a pain in the ass, but they are a lot of fun. Growing up, I had every toy imaginable. I had a large boat, jet skis, corvettes, sailboats, a motor home, airplanes and motorcycles.

Here is the problem: after a while, your girl will hate everything about your toys, because you're spending your hard-earned money to keep them working, and/or running. Women, will always bitch about all the toys; it's just a matter of time. They want you to spend the money you are spending on your toys (the things that make you happy) all on them. It's fucked up.

Guys, all toys will become a pain in the ass. Let's talk reality. A boat is a nightmare toy: It comes with a trailer that rusts, tires that rot and bearings that seize. It will kill your towing vehicle (truck), because it's so heavy. It has insurance, it has parking fees, it needs storage, it needs gas and oil, etc. It needs to be cleaned and waxed, and you only get to use it twice a year. It's fun to go fishing and take your girl boating with your friends, but in reality, it's way too costly and is a pain in the ass.

Rent a boat when you need a boat. It's always cheaper to rent. Motor homes, airplanes, and jet skis all work the same way. They all require big maintenance and repairs—and no one can fix anything in todays fucked up world, anyway. Rent, Rent, Rent. Got it

So remember, it pays to rent all of your toys when you're having that midlife crisis. I will say, that a motorcycle, is the least expensive toy that you can purchase, it requires the least amount of attention, and it is a lot of fun. Your girl will eventually hate it too, but it's nice to get on the open road, and cruise for breakfast or lunch with a friend.

Remember, if you marry your bitch, she gets all your shit in the end anyway, when you get divorced. Her new boyfriend, will love your nice toys, so you don't need to keep them clean and in perfect condition.

Rent all your toys; it's easier. Remember, if it flies, fucks or floats, you must rent it. No exceptions. Do you understand? Got it? Do you see why this book is so valuable? It will save you hundreds of thousands of dollars over your life time, if you would just follow our simple instructions. If you must get married to your bitch, be sure you use a prenuptial agreement so you can try to keep some of your shit when she hates your guts, divorces your ass, and throws your ass out the door. It's just a matter of time, for they all do it, you just don't know when. Good luck, you asshole.

15

Why Are All Women Hypersensitive?

Hyperthyroid, menopause, estrogen, progesterone, monthly periods, depression and mood swings. What the fuck is all of this shit, you ask? It's a time bomb. All I can say, is that my father never explained any of this shit to me. Every one of the items above, will be a part of your relationship with your woman, someday.

Trying to keep it all balanced, is impossible. You get to listen to all this bullshit, and how it will affect her sex drive and moods. If you just have your bitch on the rental program, you can say to her, "I have to go". That was easy.

Guys, you can only take so much of her shit per month. Every issue she has, is now your problem for life, if you choose to marry her. It seems like women go to doctors, psychiatrists, shrinks and counselors for help, and they all come back more fucked up than when they went in. This is another scam that, we as men, have to pay for. Doctors get 10 minutes of paid time to fix your girl, due to insurance restrictions, that sucks.

Doctors have very limited time to consult with your woman. Counselors and psychiatrists will see your girl every hour of every day if she wants, because they are paid by the hour in cash.

If your girl decides to go to counseling, that's when the guy finds out, that he is the reason why his bitch is all fucked up. Holy shit, it never ends. Next thing you know, is that you both have to go to counseling, and you both end up fucked up. Now, you're supporting the whole damn doctor's office financially. This shit never stops.

All men know with women, that there is your female, and/or there is your female with her hormones all out of whack Trying to reason with any female with her hormones all out of control, is like playing with a house that is on fire. Until you put the fire out (getting the hormones under control), the only thing you as a male can do is watch it burn itself out. You yourself do not have enough water or hose length, to fix this major hormonal problem. Now, that's fucked up. Guys, if your girl's hormones are out of control, be sure she understands that she is not acting properly, and needs professional help from a specialist that understands hormone replacement therapy.

The biggest problem men have is that women most of the time wants to blame everyone around them (family and friends), for their nasty and rude behavior, when they themselves are the entire problem.

That being said, ladies, if you are always irritable, have a case of the nasties, argumentative or just plain rude, be sure to take your hormonal medicine every day. Do this and you will learn how to control yourself and your behavior. Guys, same rules apply to you.

If you insist on not taking your prescribed medication, know that you are a royal pain-in-the-ass to everyone around you. Ladies, not all hormonal medicine causes cancer, get help today.

If your primary doctor does not understand hormone replacement therapy, or if he or she is too busy, be sure to contact a professional doctor that does. By doing this, you can have a life full of joy, and your man will not be so miserable being around you.

Remember ladies, just because you are in menopause, it does not give you the license to be a nasty, miserable bitch to your man. It doesn't work that way anymore, bitch. Us men are tired. Men, from this point forward, we only ride on the nice, clean, no baggage, drama free trains. Got it.

In the end, be careful of these so-called professionals. Most psychiatrists, and/or counselors work on the billable hour scam, and are only there to listen to you talk and take all your money.

Most of these professionals, are more screwed up than you. How is it that these professional jackasses, are going to help you guys if they are more fucked up than you? Answer is, they won't. Don't waste your time or money with these scamming professionals, if all you really need is a doctor that specializes and understands hormone replacement. That was easy.

16

Blood Work Is Normal, My Ass

All doctors, will tell you that your girl's blood work is normal, even though she is depressed and suffering from anxiety (possibly a form of menopause), and can't even get out of bed. Remember, just because her doctor says her blood work is fine, it might not be at the optimum level. It's kind of like running your car on low-octane gas. Your vehicle works best with good, clean, high-octane gas.

Your girl's body works the same way. Doctors, don't seem to care. As long as her blood work is within normal range, they'll tell her she is fine. Holy shit, the doctor should try living with this bitch for an hour. Are you kidding me? Fuck that shit.

Guys, have you ever heard of menopause? My marriage of 25 years ended because of this crazy shit. When a woman enters premenopause, partial menopause, menopause, or post menopause, she can be one fucked up, hormonal bitch, if she doesn't get proper help with medicine. Some women, won't go to the doctor to get help, because they blame you for all their problems, and the asshole doctor has told them their blood work is fine. Fuck you, doc.

Your girl, under some form of menopause, might become nasty, and can be a total bitch with hot flashes. Some countries don't allow, and/or put up with this kind of behavior. Why do they call this fucked up behavior menopause?

Men have nothing to do with it, other than we get cut off from the pussy, and you have to deal with it until she gets help. That's why they call it men get paused, I guess. It should be called *womenopause.* Whatever you want to call it, you're fucked until she decides to get professional medical help, and take her fucking medication. Holy shit, it never stops.

Guys, let me tell you: this is the biggest scam in the book, if your bitch doesn't get proper help. Possible symptoms of menopause, include her being tired all the time, tingling in her hands and feet, sensitivity too cold, dry skin, weight gain, thinning eyebrows, anxiety, insomnia, hot flash, headaches, migraines, inability to concentrate, wants no sex, depressed moods, itchy skin, fluid retention, low energy, fatigue, headaches, brain fog, joint and muscle pain, hair loss, constipation, nasty attitude and low body temperature. Holy crap, what the fuck is next, you ask? Are you kidding me? I never signed up for all this shit. Nobody in their right mind would ever be that stupid.

Being married to some bitch with all these symptoms is like driving an old car that is rusted out, has a bad motor, a bad transmission, and all the doors and windows are broken. Good fucking luck in getting that car to the finish line. It ain't going to happen buddy. What the fuck? I give up.

Women, when they age out, and/or get older, tend to get a nastier attitude with time. Once your women, gets a case of the nasties, long term you are done. Gentlemen, just wait, you will see what I am talking about as your beautiful women that you love dearly, gets a little older. Men, on the other hand, tend to get nicer with age and have more patience, go figure. I guess, we just give up on everyone. WTF.

17

Women Have To Bitch About Something All The Time

Women, always must bitch or nag about something; it is part of the female hormonal makeup, or DNA. Over the years, I have learned that a woman can have the perfect date, the perfect job, the perfect boyfriend or husband, but she still has to bitch or find something to bitch about. It's in her genes somewhere, I guess. What the fuck?

Women, create drama, pick arguments, and say shit just so they can have something to complain or bitch about. If ever there was one thing I could change in the world, it would be to end world hunger, and then to tell women to *shut the fuck up and stop bitching and nagging about every damn thing that is already perfect.* You wear your man, the fuck out.

You ladies, bitch so much that you ruin life for us guys. We can only put up with your shit for so long, and then we want you the fuck away from us.

Men, hate it when you nag, bitch or wine. One of the biggest pet peeves men have against women, is that women are always nagging about something. Ladies, quit nagging your man immediately, because it will eventually just make him leave. He can't take it anymore. I am putting all women on notice to stop that shit today. It is unhealthy for any relationship, and your man will just find some new ass if you don't stop.

Now, that this cat is out of the bag, and you know we are right, we men want you ladies to take the 90-Day, No Bitching/No Nagging Challenge. Try it, please. You will like it. The 90-Day, No Bitching/No Nagging Challenge is this: any time you want to open your mouth and bitch or nag about something, stop and direct all your attention to fixing your hair and applying makeup, so as to keep your little minds occupied on yourselves. Don't worry about what everyone else in the world is doing around you; just look at yourself in the mirror and tell yourself how beautiful you are. That was easy.

By doing this, all the attention is diverted to you, and your little head is preoccupied with something very positive, so you should have nothing to bitch about. Try this for 90 days, and I guarantee you will feel better about yourself, and you will stop your bitching and nagging. Women, just be happy, for you drive all of us asshole men nuts.

We as men, can't tell women how to act or behave in the 21st Century, because that would be considered some form of narcissism by female counselors. Ladies, we get it. If you want to be a nasty miserable bitch, that's ok, just leave us men the fuck alone, move the hell out, and we men will be just fine. Thank you for cooperation in advance.

18

Try Fixing Crazy Female Drama With Her Girlfriends

Your woman, has all these girlfriends, who will influence her every day. Her friends, will put shit in her little head that is just plain stupid. All her girlfriends have major problems, and they will make all their major problems, your woman's problems and fuck up your woman's little mind. Men, hate all female drama for it sucks the life right out of us.

So, ladies, if you are going to bring any kind of fucking, bull shit drama into our lives, pack your shit and get the fuck out, today. Are we clear on this? Men, would rather go get a tooth pulled than listen to all that fucked up non-sense. Ladies, stop that shit, you are wearing your little man's ass the fuck out. Thank you. We told them guys, hope it helps.

The bottom line here, gentlemen, is that if you put five women together in a room, and your woman is not all messed up yet, she will be when she leaves that room. How do you like that shit? When girls hang out together and bash men over all the shit we did or did not do, this is called a cluster fuck on steroids. Nothing good can ever come from one of these gatherings when it comes to men. Her girlfriends, have created doubt about all the things that you have told your female; all the things you might have done for her, you learn, were also done for all the wrong reasons. Fuck that shit, who cares, it's done, and it's over with.

Women, dream up more shit in their little heads in one day, that makes no sense, and confuses all of us men for the rest of our adult lives, than any other creature on the planet. All women, like to gossip about their men and there is nothing wrong with this, except that they believe in all the stupid shit that they hear. When your female gets home from her gathering, you will spend years trying to straighten out the mess that's in her head, that started with 30 minutes of stupid conversation with her girlfriends. Guys, get your lady a hobby to keep that tiny little mind of hers away from all the catty drama that all her fucked up girlfriends have.

Once her head is all fucked up by her stupid friends, it will take 101 psychologists, psychiatrists, sociologists, counselors, medical doctors, and every other fucking professional to fix her. It ain't going to happen and that shit is very expensive. Got it?

In other words, you will spend the rest of your adult life trying to fix your bitch from all that crazy female drama. Guys, I'm telling you, once her head is all fucked up, it's cheaper just to trade it in for a new model. This old horse needs to go to pasture, and you need to get a newer, younger, and sexier ride. Women, always love it when they hear that shit. That was easy. Rent.

P.S.1. Don't let the hobby that your girl likes be the same as yours. Boys, you will always need, "me" time, and that does not include any women. Do you understand?

P.S.2. One more side note: When it comes to house cleaning, laundry, washing towels, and stacking the dishwasher, guys, you will never do it right. I never knew it was that hard to do these simple tasks correctly, but apparently, these bitches are the only ones that can do anything right, for they are all geniuses. Let them fucking do it. I quit. Holy shit.

P.S.3. All women, always want what other women have. Ladies, be fucking happy with what you have. Quit worrying about all the things that other people have that do not concern you. Ladies, mind your own damn business, please. Can you do that? Is that possible? Thank you. Okay, guys, we told them. That was easy. Mission accomplished. What's next?

P.S.4. The blame game. Women, always want to blame their problems on someone else. Ladies, I am putting you on notice to take control of your problems immediately. Do not blame everyone else for your catty bullshit problems when you created them in the first place. Fess up, take control of things, and get professional help from a non-fucked-up third party. Do not blame other people for your stupid problems when you are the problem yourself. Enough said.

P.S.5. One more pet peeve that men have against you ladies: the person who pays the electric bill in your home controls the thermostat. That's it. In other words, if it's cold outside, bitch, put clothes on that are appropriate for the temperature inside the home. Ladies, men are not cheap, but it costs money to heat and cool a home. Let's use common sense when it comes to controlling the thermostat, please. If you are the last one to leave the home, adjust the thermostat accordingly so as not to waste energy and save the environment. Also, guys remember, that if your rich bitch pays the electric bill, adjust the thermostat however she wants it, because she is the boss. Got it? Enough said.

P.S.6. Shut the fucking door on the refrigerator. The refrigerator is a cooling system to keep food items cold and/or frozen. It's not meant to cool the house or the entire city in which you live in. Ladies and children, please close the door on the refrigerator once you have retrieved the items you were looking for.

By doing this, we will save energy and the environment, and the food inside the refrigerator won't spoil as fast. Ok, got it. Also, when entering and leaving one's home, always close the door behind you so as not to waste energy. Electricity is very expensive, let's not just waste it. Again, common sense.

P.S.7. Ladies, remember when your man takes you out for a nice dinner, you don't have to order one of everything on the menu. I have been out for dinner and seen families order appetisers and full meals, and then after two bites, the women and children say they are full. Ladies, stop wasting our money on food items you are not going to eat. There are people starving all around the world for Pete Sakes. What's a matter with you, oh that's right, you don't pay the food bill? I got it.

The moral of the story here is, only order the amount of food that you can eat and feel comfortable with. Remember ladies, after menopause, you need to be careful about your diet anyway, for if you are not, you will end up being the size of a Buick. Now let's not go there. Guys, same goes for you, always eat responsibly. It's called common sense.

P.S.8. Ladies, I am here to tell you that when your man takes a business phone call after hours, or at home, do not roll your eyes at him. Most businessmen make their living on their cell phones by communicating with their customers. Some customers require after-hours calls and are high maintenance, but don't forget, that these are the same pain-in-the-ass customer phone calls that make your mortgage payment, car payment, and pay for the vacations and every other damn thing you, ladies require us to provide. So next time your man receives a business phone call at dinnertime, tell him what a wonderful man he is, and thank him for providing for his family the best way he can. The End. Do you understand, bitch? Your man, is most likely doing all he can.

P.S.9. When going to bed, ladies, always take a shower, pretty yourself up, and put your man's favorite perfume on so as to make him desire you. Men like it when you wear your sexy nighties, but always remove your undergarments before retiring to bed. If you are a kind, lovable, happy person, we men love to snuggle and make love to you. By being naked, you have invited your man into your nest, and maybe some wild lovemaking will happen. If you're a nasty, miserable bitch, be sure to leave your clothes on so that we men know you are off-limits tonight, and to go elsewhere if we want to tap some ass tonight. That was easy. Guys, don't forget you need to clean up too.

P.S.10. Brushing your teeth and personal hygiene is a must. Ladies and gentlemen, always brush your teeth if you think you will be kissing on your partner soon or making love to each other. By doing this, your breath will be minty fresh when you make contact with each other's lips. Bad things can happen when your breath is nasty, so be romantic ladies and gentlemen, and brush those dam teeth. Got it.

When you first get up in the morning, brush and remove any nasties you acquired while you were sleeping. Always brush and floss your teeth after every meal. Brush the top of your tongue too, for the more you talk, the more bacteria that builds up and has to be cleaned away, it's true. Most women talk too much anyway, so brush a little longer, ladies. Lol. Remember to brush your teeth before bedtime. Nobody wants to kiss a girl or guy that has bad breath. Got it. Guys, you need to follow the same rules so as to be fair. Enough about brushing your teeth.

P.S.11. Ladies, the cooch is another item that needs to be spotless. Keep that thing clean at all times. We as men, will not tell you how to do it. Just do it. Shower that puppy in the morning and before retiring to bed. By doing this we know you are squeaky clean and ready for action.

If it is dirty, and not maintained properly, then we as men don't want to play with it. It will go into retirement and become dormant, and another open store may need to be found. Let's not let that happen. Guys, you need to keep that private area clean, too, if you want the extra special treatment, if you know what I mean. Enough said.

P.S.12. Ladies, STOP with the silent treatment when you are upset with your man. Men, are tired and have played this game with women for more than a century. Communication is the only way to discuss and resolve issues. Texting, emailing, using the silent treatment, and sleeping in another room are all part of an upset woman's defense mechanism. Men, shut down when they hear conversation that is stupid. Ladies, before you talk, make sure what you are saying makes logical sense. Think before you speak. Stop with those little digs; you know which ones I'm talking about. If you have nothing nice to say, don't say anything at all. That was easy. Men, this goes for you, too.

Remember ladies, what comes out of your mouth can never be taken back. Apologize quickly when you know you have said something that you did not mean, and/or was hurtful. If you are just plain mad, be sure to communicate with your partner as soon as you have calmed down. Bottom line, communication is the most important part of a relationship. Never engage in heavy conversation to fix a problem in your relationship, if you are under the influence of alcohol, drugs, and/or are not taking your medication. But in the end, ladies, if you must give us the silent treatment, and you're still going to give us pussy, we as men are okay with your behavior of being quiet. That works too. We like that.

P.S.13. Women, always ask the question, "Why"? Why are you going here? Why are you doing it that way? Why do you have to go? Ladies, stop asking "why" on everything!

This behavior drives men crazy. We as men, never ask our ladies "why" on anything. We just don't. We do not care why you girls do what you do. Men know women are going to do things that we will never understand, but over the years we have learned to keep our fucking mouths shut.

The past is the past, and we understand as a male, that we cannot fix the past. So, from this point forward, do not ask your man, "Why"? We are tired of hearing it. Ladies, if you ask us, "Why" from this point forward, we are putting you on notice that the only answer we will respond with is, "Because". Got it? Discussion is over. We don't care.

P.S.14. With today's females, gentlemen, you cannot give help, give advice, assist, aid, guide, evaluate, modify anything with women today, for they all get mad, upset, pissed off, aggravated, go psychotic, become unhinged, get disturbed, go belligerent, or just plain go crazy. I don't give a dam who the fuck you thing you are, women in today's world know everything, and you male assholes are just in their way. We get it. It's all about you females, in today's America.

Ladies, how about the next time we have a communication error (argument) in our relationship, you shut the fuck up for the next 30 seconds, and just listen to what I have to say without you opening your mouth. You think you could do that, please? By doing this new exercise, we might even be able to communicate and understand each other. Guys, this might even work both ways? Communication is a must; Colonel Smoke, is teaching people how to communicate every day. Sometimes it just pays to shut the fuck up and listen. Remember, GOD gave us two ears and one mouth. Listen twice as much as you talk. That was easy.

The 21st Century mans creed is; I solemnly swear that all women are all geniuses, and all men are just pieces of shit and can be shit on by all women, 24 hours a day. So, men, now that we know where we stand in society, relax, chill, and have fun, tap some good ass, and always drink the best cold beer you can find. The cool think about this manuscript is that it is guaranteed to save, and/or end the relationship that you currently have now. Remember, if she reads the most powerful book in the world and comprehends its content, you might even have a keeper on your hands and have to get married. WTF. That's some shit, right.

P.S.15. When it comes to telling your little man something, ladies don't tell your man the same thing 17 times over, and over again. Men, here their women the first time you say something, this does not mean we are going to listen to what you have to say. We men, do things are own way. American women are always right, but we men don't really give a shit. So, ladies, please tell your man something once and then let it go. Let's not beat a dead horse to death, for it does no good. Ladies, whatever you do, please do not repeat yourself 17 times on the same fucking thing. Got it. Is that ok? Now, let's be nice to each other and move the fuck on. That was easy.

P.S.16. Men, have learned over the years when a woman says, "yes" it does not necessarily mean yes, and when she says, "no" it does not always mean, no. Women also say, "I don't care," but in reality, they do. All this wacky communication makes it very complicated for men to understand women. We have no fucking idea what you meant, by what you said.

Ladies, from this point forward, please say what you really mean, so your man will not be confused. Men know that in the end, women will be upset regardless of what you say and how you react. Men have learned that pleasing emotional women is next too impossible. It can't be done. That being said, the next time you ladies answer with, "yes", "no", "maybe", or "I don't car", please put it in writing so both of us know and understand what you meant. That was easy. Now that makes sense.

Now, that men have explained some of the problems we have had with our women over the years, we are drawing a line in the sand. If you ladies would just follow these simple instructions you just learned in this chapter, we men agree to lift the toilet seat up every time, when we pee and we will put the seat down when we are done, so you women don't fall in. It's a small price to pay, but us men are standing united on this one, and now you women have won the toilet seat battle. It's called a compromise, and us men are here, able, and we are willing to do all this to make all you women happy. Life is so simple; once you understand what women want. LOL.

19

Women, Stop With The Attitude

American women of the 21st century, seem to all have attitude and think their shit don't stink. Ladies, I am here to tell you: your shit does stink. Your attitude tells us guys if we want to be around you. Don't cop an attitude every time you don't get your way bitch; men are tired of your shit.

American D.I.V.A girl- Dominating, Intense, Vicious, Attitude girl- Do you have one of these? Diva girls are hot, sexy and expensive. They bitch and wine all the time, and everything is always all about them. Diva girls do not cook or clean and they think they are above all the rest of us. I am here to tell you; you are dead wrong.

Diva girls are great for one night stands, and they will rock your world and make you feel like you are one big swinging dick, but trust me, long term, they are just a big pain in the ass. Diva girls only qualify for the four F's, in the manual and are not considered long term relationship material. Diva girls are way too expensive. Ride a Diva girl today, and then let them go tomorrow, cowboy. You will be glad you did.

To all you Diva's out there. The moral of this manuscript is, if you are going to be nasty, disrespectful and ungrateful, you got's to go. Be nice or get the hell out. We men, are not going to renegotiate a peace treaty every time you Diva's don't get your way. See that was easy. Gentlemen, we told them again, maybe this time they understand?

Today, we guys know those crazy looks that you give us daily: rolling your eyes, talking behind our backs, and cutting off the pussy, because you can. Okay, we hear you loud and clear. If you ladies are going to always have a nasty attitude, we guys are just going to ride another trolley. There is a new trolley every five minutes, bitch, so there. Now we solved that problem, too. What the hell is next?

Women, don't like the word, "no" for some reason. All these bitches think they are entitled to everything, no you're not. Ladies, I am putting you on notice today, that the world does not always have to revolve around you. If it's your money and your time, then ladies it's probable going to be your way. But if it's your man's money, and his time, then it's probable going to be his way and he might tell you, "no" from time to time. This is called common fucking sense. Ladies, does this make any sense to you?

The bottom line here is to always remember, whoever pays the freight is the driver of the car. Ladies, the stewardess does not fly the plane. The pilot flies the plane, or it would crash. Ladies, quit trying to be the fucking pilot when you're not. The End. Got it. Do I have to say any more? I think we made it clear. Ladies, just be nice and everything will be just fine. Guys, you need to be nice too.

Always remember, that you are not the only piece of ass available, so drop your attitude, and try to be pleasant the next time you're with your little man, and he might even treat you like a lady if you qualify and deserve it. Got it. Your man will love you twice as much if you don't have an attitude. Try it, you might like it. Ladies, smile once and awhile, and I promise you might even feel better about yourself. That's pretty simple. Guys, you think your woman gets it?

20

Ladies, Stop Your Lying Today

Ladies, stop your lying today. We guys know that half the shit that comes out of your mouth is either a lie, or stretching the real story. Ladies, you're now put on notice, that we understand your trickery, and we are sick of your lying, cheating, scamming ways.

So next time, just tell the fucking truth, and quit making shit up all the time. Can you do that for us, please? Ladies, thank you for your cooperation in advance. Your man would be truly grateful, enough Said.

21

Women Don't Need To Know Everything

The reason guys don't tell women everything about our personal and work lives is because you females can't handle it. That's right: we tell you a situation, and you then get stupid, or say stupid shit to blow everything out of proportion. It's all bullshit.

Women, make all your problems their problems. They know all the answers to your shit, even when they don't understand the situation, and/or the question. How the hell can you know everything about everything, and have all the right answers to a situation that took years to develop, when you don't even understand the question?

Ladies, I am telling you nicely, that sometimes it pays to just shut the fuck up and just be quiet. As all guys know, you ladies want to know everything in your guys' heads. That shit ain't going to happen. Stay out of our heads please, and quit manipulating shit that you don't understand.

Guys, don't tell everything to your bitch that you don't want the whole world to know. She won't understand the situation and she sure can't fix it, so keep your fucking mouth, shut. That was easy. Problem solved. Colonel Smoke, (The Master) knows everything about women, and now he has saved your little ass. Look what you just learned, you asshole. Shut the fuck up and be happy.

Ladies and boredom do not mix either. Ladies, when you are bored, please don't bother your man by asking him a stupid question, like why are you doing that? When are you going to mow the grass? How are you going to fix the car? When are you washing my car? Ladies, stop, get yourself a second job if you have to, and quit worrying about all the things your little man is doing all day.

Ladies, if you are just plain bored, make yourself up pretty, put on your favorite dress, pick up a nice book, or magazine and occupy yourself without bothering your little man. Men get tired of answering all of your little questions, and trying to entertain their women throughout their adult life. Also, guys, if you catch yourself being bored, find something constructive to do and leave your little women alone. It works both ways. Got it, enough said.

22

Honey, What Are You Doing Today?

Why do women always ask what we're going to do today when we leave for work? Ladies, men hate this shit. What do you think I am going to do today, bitch? I am going to work today. I love my job, I love my boss, and I am going to make my boss a bunch of money, so we can eat and be merry.

Or would you like to hear, that I have two hookers ordered, I'm going boating with them, they are going to be naked, and I'm going to be on my best behavior? Enough said. Honey, would you like to go boating with us today? Guys, it's all bullshit. Just ignore it, and let it go like a kidney stone. It's all painful. WTF.

Ladies, don't ask stupid questions when your man is going to his job to bust his ass and make a paycheck for his family. Think before you ask a stupid question. From here on out, he is going to give you a stupid answer. So next time your man is leaving for work, just tell him how much you love him, and that you're praying for him to have a fantastic, money making day. That's it. If he is doing something that he is not supposed to be doing, he will just lie to you anyway, so as to prevent an argument.

Ladies, if you take care of your man and are nice, he will make all the right decisions. If you are a nag, or a bitch, he will just be gone all the time. Control your nagging, ladies.

23

Men Love It When You Smile

Ladies, if you're listening, you should smile every once-in-a while. Guys, love it when a lady smiles and shows a little bit of positive affection. When you smile, you bring joy to most people who see you. Everyone loves a smile.

It has been proven that it takes fewer muscles to smile than it does to frown and look miserable. So, ladies, if you're looking to date a nice guy, get rid of your attitude and always wear a smile on your face. You will notice the difference immediately. That was easy. Can you do that for us, pretty please? We thank you so very much in advance.

24

Cheaper To Keep Her

Guys, I am here to tell you that finding the perfect woman, a woman who is going to take care of you and the family every day, and not bitch or do shit to piss you off, is not going to happen in today's world. So if you are married already, did not have a chance to read this book, and you are feeling the pain, let me give you some averages.

There are seven days to a week. If you are happily married five out of the seven days per week, then you should just sit tight, enjoy the best ride you can, and count all your blessings every day. This means that 71.42857% of the time, your girl is bringing joy into your life, and that she is only sucking the life out of you 28.51142% of the time. Not bad, right.

These percentages are considered good in today's world. Guys, on the other hand, if you are in a relationship and every day is less joyful than the day before, you may have to ask yourself this question: "Do I work on this relationship to change my girl to the way I would like for her to be, or do I just put up with all the non-sense".

Remember, guys, this is called, "narcissistic" by the female counselors if you try to explain how you would like your girl to act. It's hard to figure that drug, alcohol, and spending addictions are considered narcissistic behavior, or that you're a control freak, when you're in a relationship with someone and trying to help her. It's all bullshit. This is when you know shit is all fucked up in the world.

My advice: you can try to help someone with their addictions, at least once, but if it backfires and blows up in your face, you might have to move on. In life, one always has to try to save a relationship, but if one person of the two wants nothing to do with doing the right thing, and does not want to change for the better, then I'm telling you that fixing the relationship is not going to happen.

If the pursuit of happiness of your relationship does not outweigh the pain, then you need to talk to your partner. Relationships are either improving or getting worse with time. If you can't grow and be a better person every day with the relationship you're in, get the hell out. Always be growing, don't quit and be positive. Got it?

If you're married, and in a relationship, that consists of fighting, arguing, shouting, and there is no peace, get the fuck out, for it's not a healthy environment. I know so many people who stay in unhealthy situations and are miserable their entire lives. Guys, life is short, and we are only here for a blink of an eye. Enjoy every day you get out of bed; for one day, you will not get up. Remember men, always be respectful to your lady.

Ladies, part of being a beautiful woman, is taking care of your guys needs, every day. Your man needs sex every day, or at least have the option for it, even if you are not in the mood. If there is a nuclear war going on in your relationship with your man, he still needs ass. A guys' needs must be taken care of or we just leave and find some new ass. We will not argue any longer. That's all.

All men need to have a great piece of ass if you want them to hang around and be with you. You ladies have needs and so does your man. So, now that we have learned that men and women have needs, it's time that both genders realize if this relationship is going to last long term, then all of us must work together. Respect is another thing that men must have, or we are just going to be gone. Women don't seem to understand, like we said earlier, we just don't give a shit any longer. That's it.

So, ladies, the bottom line here is, if you decide that you are not going to give your man ass or take care of his needs, then pack your shit and move the fuck out. That was easy. Guys, I think we told them, if only they would just listen. Some of the women out their will get it. Some will, some won't, so what. It is what it is. THE END. Enough said, have a nice day. WTF.

25

Internet Dating Sites Are Where It's At Today

Dating today, is easier than ever. Remember the saying, "There is a new train every few minutes coming to you"? The trains today are called Internet dating sites, and they make it so much easier to meet people and find a date. Social media sites are also fantastic dating machines. All these sites are full of people looking to find the right connections and/or hook-ups.

So, if you're single, married, and/or you want to be single, go on the Internet, and I promise, that you will meet people who are looking for love or a date. It may take 100 dates or conversations to find the right person who has the qualities you're looking for, but they're out there, and be sure to never stop looking until you find what you are looking for.

Some people get upset when they go on a few dates, and it doesn't work out; they say the dating sites don't work. Guys, it is the law of averages that works in our favor. One out of 10 dates will be good and one out of 100 will be fantastic, so go find a fantastic date who makes you happy and be sure to enjoy every minute of every day. *Meeting for coffee is always a good way to meet a new person to see if there is any chemistry.*

Remember guys, women who are on dating sites are telling you they are available to have fun, party, go clubbing, movies, dinner, and may even want to get laid. What's wrong with that? Life is all about having a good time and sharing it with someone you care about. Dating sites make it a whole lot easier than going to a bar trying to find out who wants to mingle, and who does not in your local area.

You may not find love on every date, or get laid for that matter. You will meet new friends, that have friends, that knows somebody that has more friends. Get it, just have fun, and go meet lots of new people, you will be glad you did. The world is now your oyster. Go get 'em tiger, and play the game till you find the one who makes you happy. That was easy. Remember, the music of life never stops until your dead.

So live life every day like it is your last day, and I promise you, you will have a more fulfilling and happier life than you ever imagined. Always keep it simple when dating, and quit falling in love with every piece of ass you tap. Enough about dating.

26

A Woman's Algorithm

If you could figure out a woman's algorithm, you would be a fucking genius. Can you imagine trying to figure out how the female mathematical algorithm works and what makes a woman tick? Holy shit, guys, it can't be done because when you think you have that crazy shit all figured out, it will change like the wind. Most guys, have quit trying to figure out what's in the heads of women. We're tired, worn the fuck out, and exhausted from all of their crazy unpredictability. Ladies, you win. It's all about you. You get to deal with all your girl's bullshit and then you die. What the fuck is up with that, it never ends.

A beautiful woman to a guy, is a lady that is hot, sexy, sweet, kind, smart, lovable, she takes care of her body, she can cook, she can keep a clean house, she understands a budget, she like sex, and she gives her man all the attention that he needs, if you know what I mean. She does not nag, bitch or wine about all the shit that you do wrong. Men, need support and kind words just like our ladies, or we just run the other direction and look elsewhere to find love. That was easy. Does everyone now understand how this is supposed to work?

Now, you ladies know what your man is looking for in a woman, you can try to better yourself and work on improving the relationship with the one you love. Ladies, always remember, if you don't take care of your man, some other pretty lady will. It's that simple. Guys, all women now know what we need from them for we just told them. Good luck with that shit. That was easy.

27

Women Call Them Addictions, Men Call Them Enjoyment

Some women, for some reason, think that if you smoke a cigarette you are a drug addict. If you have a beer, you're an alcoholic. If you have a gun, you are a terrorist, and if you like sex, that too is a crime and you're a sex addict and should be punished. Guys, I'm here to tell you, it's all bullshit.

Most of the time these are not addictions, it's what men like to do for enjoyment. The real story here, is that men like to do things that make them happy. That's pretty simple, go figure.
Ladies, please leave us men the fuck alone, and let us do what we want to do, for it brings joy to our lives. Thank you. Guys, I now told them and put them on notice. That's all we can do.

Females, can you please quit your nagging and bitching about all the shit that we men like to do, and just be thankful that we try to provide for our families. Your man just wants to have a little fun. Got it? It's all okay. Everything is going to be just fine. Ladies, let it all go. This is why all women need to work outside the home, so they have something to occupy their little minds. If you are busy at work, there is less time to bitch about something your man did. Just making a point, don't fly off the handle, now ladies. It's all good. Guys, stop your bitching, too.

28

Women Are Always Right

Men, I am here to tell you that women think they are always right. Women of today, like I expressed earlier, think they know everything about everything. For some reason, they think they are all geniuses. This is something new in the last 10 years, women's lib bull shit, I guess.

Here is how this works. As a guy, you can only handle so much stupid conversation from your bitch, a day. I suggest you let her be right, as long as it will not cost you anything financially. If it is going to cost you money, stop, give her kudos, then divert and change the subject to something else. Changing the subject, diverting the conversation normally works. The old way—correcting the bitch every time she is wrong—will just lead to arguments and no pussy. Now, that's fucked-up, don't be that stupid.

Relationships today, are like negotiating a peace treaty with a foreign country every minute of every day, just to get laid. The women of today have got it all fucked up; everything is a compromise and it's all about them. No, it should not be this way, but I am sorry to inform you, that it is. If you don't compromise with your woman on everything in today's world, it is called being narcissistic. That's just fucked up, too. You will either wear the pants in a relationship, or turn into a pussy depending on how much energy you want to spend on getting booty. We strongly suggest you be a man, and grow some balls. Make your momma proud.

My father's generation, would have never put up with any of the shit that women put us through today. It just wouldn't happen. Now, remember, guys: if your woman brings home the big bacon, "she is the money tree", let her be the genius. When having a stupid conversation with your super-rich woman, the money makes the conversation sound less stupid. That works. Men, don't forget that money talks and bullshit walks. If you're lucky enough to have a rich bitch, guys, shut the fuck up and let her drive the car, she is the boss. Got it? Have any questions? That was easy.

Ladies, if you're listening, you don't always have to be right and act like you always know everything. Just relax sometimes. It pays to be quiet, be nice, be polite, and just listen. You don't always have to pretend to know everything. Just because your man asks you to shut the hell up, does not mean he has anger management problems. Just because he raised his voice at you, does not mean he is a narcissist fuck, or has a temper. He is just trying to get you to listen and be quiet. He already knows, you are a genius and you know everything.

By the way, we are not going to counseling for this bullshit to learn how to control our anger, or to learn how to be more graceful when explaining to our wonderful female how we need to be more considerate of her feelings and less abusive. Fuck all that shit. We are done talking. I just explained to you for the last time how this train is going to roll… Are you on board, or are you getting the fuck off. Let me know, for this train is leaving the station now. What's your answer, got to go? THE END.

29

Scorned Women Are No Good To Any Of Us Men

If you should ever encounter a scorned woman, run as fast as you can. Do not pass go. Do not collect your $200.00 dollars. Just run Forest, run. You cannot fix this shit. Have you ever heard the saying, "Hell hath no fury like a woman scorned"? Holy shit—they are not kidding. Scorned women are downright nasty, vindictive, and just plain mean. These bitches, are no good to any of us. Women, if you are like this and you are reading our book, get professional and medical help immediately. Call an ambulance or 911.

Most women that are scorned, hate men and have all kinds of emotional problems. They have all kinds of fucked up opinions about men, and are very negative people. Holy shit, watch the fuck out for these bitches. Their only purpose in life is to ruin your life. Stay the fuck away from any scorned, crazy, fucked up, hormonal, nasty bitch. They are nuts. Got it.

Scorned, crazy bitches say shit that never happened. They make up things all the time to make themselves look like the victims. They're always telling lies. I promise you, you cannot fix this behavior at any cost. It can't be done. Get over it, and move the fuck on. Do you understand? I hope you learned something from this chapter. If you get stuck with a crazy bitch like the one we described above, just jump from any bridge or tall building, and your whole life will become easier. Lol.

30

Books, Magazines, TV, And Your Women

Women, believe all the shit they see in books, magazines, and on the television. This crap is all fiction and most of this shit is make-believe. Soap operas, real housewife's TV, fill women's heads with fantasy romances, nice cars, big houses, nice dinners, romantic bedroom scenes, and lots of hot sex. Hey ladies, this is called acting and 99% of this shit will never happen to you. Wake the fuck up, you women see all this crazy behavior, and now you want to live it. Remember bitch, that shit costs money; since we don't have any money, forget it. It's not realistic. Do you understand?

Books, are another fucked up, make-believe scam that fill women's heads with concepts and ideas that are not true and will never happen. Women read these books, wherein some famous asshole says, "this is how shit works" and women believe all this bullshit.

Ladies, I am here to tell you that half the shit you read in your fantasy, and/or self-help/love story books, is all bullshit. Quit living your life in a fantasy. Get back to reality and move the fuck on. Your dreaming has worn your man's ass, the fuck out. Okay?

Magazines, are another headache for us men. Women read them and believe all that shit in them is true, too. Holy fuck—how are we, as working stiffs, ever going to get our girl's head on straight if everything she sees is bullshit fantasy? Guys, I am here to tell you that policing your bitch, keeping her head pointed in the right direction, is a full-time job. Good fucking luck.

Now, that we have put to bed the fantasy and scam lifestyles that are all fake, let's get back to work and enjoy the lives we do have. As a guy, the only thing you hope for every day, is that you wake up, your car starts, you don't get fired from your job, you get some booty, and that your bitch has dinner on the table when you get home. That's it, very simple.

So women, please back off the fantasy lifestyle, and let's get back to reality and enjoy what we have before it too, is all gone. Life is very short, we as men just want to enjoy every day we are able to get out of bed, so let's live within our means and everything will be just fine. The End, got it.

31

Don't Spoil Your Bitch

By spoiling your bitch, you have created a monster. Guys, this is true: the more you give, the more addicted women become and they expect more all the time. If you keep raising the bar, you will eventually sink your own ship. I have seen this so many times: men buy their ladies expensive cars, expensive jewelry, expensive clothes, and suddenly, the woman changes overnight and you have a nightmare on your hands. Once you start this pattern of giving, you're fucked. These females expect bigger and better gifts each, and every year, until you die. Guys, it's not possible. Eventually all women, will be ungrateful and unappreciative about everything you do. They all do it; it's just a matter of time. Don't fucking do it! Are you sure you understand, gentlemen?

If you start washing her car, expect to do it every week. If you do the dishes, expect to do it all the time. If you start giving your girl flowers every week, the first time you don't give her flowers, you're an asshole, or she thinks you have a girlfriend. Fuck all that bull shit. Here's a daisy, bitch, enjoy it. Remember, when you first do these good deeds, women are very thankful, but once they are accustomed to this behavior and you stop, you now are a gigantic, piece of shit. Do not ever start to do anything that you're not prepared to do for the rest of your adult life. That was easy.

So, if you have learned anything here, always be respectful, but do not give expensive gifts, and/or go crazy with your gift giving, for it will always fuck you in the end. It's just a matter of time. Do you understand?

All gifts should be small and affordable, and never raise the bar, or your bitch's head will get swelled up with her ego and her hormones. Do you understand? Don't fuck it up for the next guy who has to put up with her shit. Remember, you will not be the last guy, trust me on this one. Got it?

Guys, if you raise the bar, the price of pussy will go up for all of us. Now, they *all* expect more, you asshole. Don't do it. As in life, you are going to have good and bad earning years. Women, do not understand economics. All they care about is that you are getting them expensive gifts. There are going to be times when you will not be able to afford expensive gifts, due to unforeseen circumstances, or maybe a down economy. Stop that crazy shit.

So remember, do what's expected but don't go crazy buying her expensive shit, that will be used against you for the rest of your adult life and maybe even used against you in a court of law (divorce). Once you create this monster machine, it's your pain in the ass, until death. Luckily, you will die someday, and then all this crazy shit stops. Enough said. Do you get it?

Ladies, always remember to thank your little man for all the wonderful gifts that he gives you, even though it may not have been what you wanted. It's the thought that counts bitch, don't ever forget that. Got it? Please, and thank you are pretty cool too, use them often. Try it ladies; your little man would really appreciate it, I promise. Men, be sure to give nice gifts that have meaning, no vacuums, pots and pans or cleaning supplies, please. See ladies, we told him.

32

Women Think All Men Are Narcissistic

Narcissism is bullshit. Everyone uses this word when they don't like what they hear from someone above them, or they did not get their way. Parents are the bosses of the home. You kids, get over it. The one who pays the bills in the house, is the fucking boss. My money, my time, my way, that's it, got it, that was easy. Ladies, you can always be the boss, go make some big, fucking money and you are the king. He or she that makes the fucking money, is the fucking boss. That's just the way it works. Younger women, for some reason, in this United States of America, can't understand these fucking rules. They all want to take charge and be the boss all the time. Fuck that shit. At work, if you are an employee, and your boss asks you to do something, just do it with a positive attitude and a smile. He or she is not a control freak; they are the boss. Just do what's asked of you, and everything will be just fine. Got it.

Female counselors, have misused the word narcissism for years, when they've talked about how husbands tell their wives how certain things will be done in the home. That's called narcissism today. That's bullshit. That's called *me, the breadwinner of this house, will tell you what to do and how it will operate.* What's wrong with that? That's all, no problem here. Ladies, if you're the big bread winner of your house, then guys, your bitch, is the boss. Shut the fuck up and be happy. That's it. Now that we got that shit all straightened out, life will be so easy.

Over the years, women have gotten this all fucked up. Men, if they are the bread winner, are the kings of their homes, and everyone needs to know the laws. The king makes the rules and sets the order of the house. This shit is so easy, if everyone would just follow the fucking rules. Remember, if your bitch is the breadwinner, and makes good money, then she is the fucking king of your house, and she is the fucking boss.

If you want to take over the kingdom, you better get a good paying fucking job, you asshole. If your girl pays for your house, and pays for your car, then shut the fuck up and do as the little lady says. That's pretty simple. Don't fuck this up, guys.

Everyone would love to have some rich bitch that makes a pile of money, and takes good care of her man. This is called a pipe dream and it's not going to happen to your ass, so get back to work, you asshole. When your little man raises his voice to explain a situation, or tells you no, it is not called narcissism, you crazy bitch. He raised his voice to you, and told you no, that's it, nothing else has to be discussed. Why did he raise his voice to you, you ask? A, you were either talking over him and not listening, or B, you were yelling at him and did not understand something that he was trying to explain. Ladies, listen up, just be nice and humble yourself, and everything will be just fine, Got It.

Gentlemen, you need to do the same. One percent of you truly narcissistic fucks (men), have ruined it for all of us non-narcissistic jackasses. Because of your bullshit, women think that all men are narcissistic when we tell our women what to do and how we want it done.

Ladies, let me explain one last time: The person who makes the bacon, brings home the bacon, cooks the fucking bacon, is the fucking boss. Do you get it, or do you need me to explain it to you one more time, bitch? Guys, always remember to shut the fuck up, if your lady is the bread winner. Got it.

I think it's clear now. I hope you can understand this very simple formula. This chapter was really hard for you ladies, to understand, I'm sure. I know, Colonel Smoke, tries to make it all so simple. Ladies relax, we are all learning something here. What the fuck, let it go. Remember ladies, us men are still running the, "keeper test" on your ass, so you better be nice.

33

Women Can Be Nasty And Greedy

Some women, must have the nasty gene embedded in them; being nice is a real challenge for them at times. Some women, have a tendency to be nasty and ungrateful. For some reason, women think the world revolves around them. Women, I am here to tell you, that the world does not always have to revolve around you. The only thing that you control is the pussy. That's it, and all men, because of Colonel Smoke, know this today. We get it. We guys are getting smarter every day, and we have put up with your shit for a long time. Ladies, don't be nasty or pop an attitude every time you don't get your way. Be sure to take your medicine every day, be polite, and be respectful to your man. Now, that makes common sense.

We as men, work hard. We listen to all our woman's fucked up problems as best we can. We try to fix everything for everyone. But from here on out, ladies, I am putting you all on notice. Do not cop a nasty attitude; don't belittle or embarrass us among our friends. Be sure not to treat your man like shit, because I'm going to tell you the one thing that most men don't have the balls to say to you ladies, "Go fuck yourself if you're going to be nasty, miserable bitch". Guys, we done told them, Its ok.

Men, have had it with your conceited, nasty, bitchy attitudes, and we are not putting up with that shit anymore. If you are going to be a nasty, miserable, bitch, then get the fuck out. That was easy. I think we made that clear enough, gentlemen.

Have you ever been around some crazy bitch that is bipolar? That shit, is bat, shit crazy. Bipolar disorder, people go from manic highs, to extreme depressions in less than a minute. Some women use this excuse to be one, nasty, crazy bitch. Don't let this shit take over your life, take your fucking medicine as prescribed ladies and gentlemen. Just because you are bipolar, it does not give you the right to be one, crazy, nasty lunatic. In Saudi Arabia, there is no such thing is bipolar disease. They correct all this shit with tar and feathers, and stoning. Good fucking luck. Remember guys, if you are bipolar, be sure to get medical help, too.

Women, have stolen more money from men than any other creature on earth. That's right: women have stolen and connived money from men over the last century like never before. This could be through alimony, child support, marital settlements, a business sale, legal issues, etc. In today's world, everything is all about money and power. Women, have stolen money from men and they have the power to do so, for they control the pussy. I am here to tell all the ladies of the world, that this shit is about to end. We don't fucking care anymore. How do you like that shit?

Men today, understand your scamming and conniving ways, and we are putting you on notice, that we don't give a damn anymore. Ladies, don't forget that the world does not revolve around you. We understand you bitches, and we men have little respect for you and/or your pussy if you're going to be nasty. Act like a lady, and we might decide to treat you like a lady. Until then, you have to earn that right, it's not free bitch.

Guys, another avenue for finding a nice lady is by going overseas to other countries. Asian, Japanese, Thailand, Philippine, and Russian women are mostly from loving and caring families. They cook, they clean, and they have manners and morals and have never been poisoned by the American girls.

They take care of their men like Kings, and are mostly happy with the little things in life. So if the American woman have worn your ass the fuck out with all their nasty attitudes and disrespect, try another country. You might be glad you did. Go get'em tiger.

Women today, pass judgment on everyone else, but forget to look at themselves in the mirror. Enough is enough, and we men are absolutely tired of it. Ladies are experts in passing judgment of others. Don't look elsewhere to criticize and degrade someone, when you yourself are a mess. Moral of the story here ladies, is to worry about yourself only, and not to criticize everyone else or blame others for all your screw-ups and/or mistakes. Most of the time you ladies have issues yourself that will take years to resolve. Work on becoming more positive person every day. You will be glad you did. The less you respond to negative people, the more peaceful your life will be, I guarantee it.

By reading this book, if you only change one thing in your life to become a better and more positive person, then this book was a success. Don't forget ladies: it is never too late to become a nicer person. Men, don't care about the past. They only care about the future. Take positive steps every day to be a kinder, more lovable lady. You will be glad you did. It will change your life and you will find all kinds of new friends you did not even know you had. Nobody wants to be around nasty, miserable people. Let's move forward and be happy.

34

Do Women Ever Stop Drinking?

When women start to drink, almost all the time, they can't stop and they get stupid. If you try to stop them from drinking, they get nasty and want to fight with you. There is no way to change this behaviour, except to leave whatever gathering you're at. If you don't leave, she will embarrass you amongst friends and you will have to apologize to all of your acquaintances the next day. That's fucked up. Women, act stupid when they get drunk. Men get happy or angry. Ladies and gentlemen, if you have a drinking problem, get help immediately.

Being the watchdog over your girl's drinking is only going to piss her off. You are in a no-win situation when trying to control someone else's drinking. If your girl gets all fucked up, the night's a bust. You do not get laid, and she can't understand why you're pissed off at her. You can also try diversion when it comes to her drinking too much; it sometimes works. Have her eat more, dance, go for a walk, or worse yet, leave the party, hopefully with her. Women, the number one rule is this: don't get drunk and embarrass your male partner among his friends. Got it? If your bitch is all fucked up, it might be a good time to find a new piece of ass. Hell, your girl won't even remember tomorrow anyway. What the fuck? Girls, the moral of the story is this: drink responsibly, or don't drink at all. If you have a drinking problem, get help. Whatever you do, do not drink and drive, otherwise someone is going to get killed. Alcoholics Anonymous does a great job of helping people with drinking problems. Enough said. Gentlemen, this goes for you, too.

35

Boob Jobs: Why Are Women Never Happy With Their Bodies?

Women, are never happy with their bodies. They're always looking at other women, and trying to outdo each other. Bigger boobs, bigger butts, tummy tucks, saggy cheeks—guys, there is no comment you can say when your woman asks about surgery to her body. Everything she asks is a loaded question; you will never win this battle. Just tell her how beautiful she is in your eyes, and move the fuck on.

Worst case: create a diversion and change the subject. The longer you talk about her body, the faster your ship will sink and you will not get any booty. Women, need to relax when it comes to keeping up with all the younger, hotties. Sagging boobs, wider hips, and saggy skin is all part of the aging process. Drink less, eat right, work out, take care of yourself and your body will be just fine.

Ladies, you make all of us men tired when all you talk about is your aging, old body. I have an idea. Let's enjoy whatever time we have left on the planet, for one of these days, it will all be gone anyway. How about that? That's genius.

36

Jealous Women Are Nuts

Jealousy, is a woman thing, I guess. Guys, women get jealous when you look, talk to, or even acknowledge another woman. I have never understood this behavior, but all women do it. If this ever happens, your woman does one of two things. She may cling to you immediately and want to fuck your brains out right there and then to let you know that she is yours and not to forget it, or she turns into a nasty, miserable bitch. She will cut off the pussy and she will make you beg for it, and then she treats you like shit for two days. If the latter one happens, your bitch has got to go. Remember; don't forget, the next train is always right around the corner and men never beg for pussy. That was easy.

Ladies, control yourself when your man is talking to another beautiful woman. Most men, are just being polite to a woman when they meet her for the first time. It's called "being courteous". So, ladies, control your jealous rages; if you don't, your man will be gone. Remember ladies, men do not beg for booty any longer. We just move the fuck on, and catch the next train, so please don't cut us off or we will just go elsewhere. Got it? Do you understand? Ladies, with that being said, control your emotions at all times. If you see a woman who is pretty and is talking to your man, be nice, be polite, be classy and always take the high road. Show her what kind of lady you truly are. Your male companion is just trying to be nice. Also, in the business world today, your man is going to meet beautiful ladies every day. Take care of your man behind closed doors, and I promise you, he will be committed to you. Remember ladies, no nagging or bitching, or you got's to go. That's all. Got it? That was easy. Same goes for you, guys.

37

Driving A Car: Why Can't Women Use Turn Signals?

When going someplace with your significant other, always take the initiative and be the driver. The best way to wreck a relationship, is by letting your bitch drive you. First of all, it's embarrassing to most guys. Most guys think that when people see them in the passenger seat in a car, they just got out of jail, or they have no driver's license. Just take charge and drive. The other reason you want to drive is that your girl never knows where she is going. She's on the gas, she's on the brakes and you're about to get whiplash. Holy Shit. Stop the fucking car and let me drive, dam it.

Also, women always put their makeup on, do their hair, do their nails when they're driving the car. It drives men nuts, stop that crazy shit. Who's driving the car? There is a time and place to do all this, it's called the fucking bathroom. Get up earlier and get prepared for your day. Stay off Facebook when driving, you are going to kill someone. Lastly, always wear your shoes when driving. If you must make a hard stop for some reason, you can't push on the brake hard enough with no shoes. Enough said.

Try explaining to your significant other that her vehicle is equipped with turn signals—and convince her that she needs to try to use them without pissing her off. If you can do this one simple task and explain to her how much safer she would be on the road, all men in America would be grateful. Good luck; it ain't going to happen.

Ladies, when your man is driving the car, please don't start whining or nagging him. Car riding is a great time to have a little quiet time. Women, have to tell us everything that is happening on the road in front of us, and always have to comment on our driving. You are either going too fast, too slow, or you need to move over. Ladies, shut the hell up for Pete Sake's. Don't give us any directions for you have no idea where you are going either, unless we ask. It just starts an argument. So ladies, just relax and enjoy the view out the window and everything will be just fine. Can you do that? Thank you, ladies, for your cooperation in advance.

You're never going to get laid if you argue with your girl about her driving, and/or using turn signals. So, gentlemen, shut the hell up. Take charge and drive, and you have a better chance of getting nookie tonight.

38

Dream Stealing: Why Do Women Steal Our Dreams?

Don't let people, and/or your girl steal your dreams, or suck the energy out of you. Family, friends, and girlfriends will always want to steal your dreams. This can't happen. People always want to give you advice and tell you why things won't work. Successful people never listen to the naysayers. We just don't.

Take charge if you have an idea, invention, or business opportunity and you really want to see if it will work. Make a road map, set some deadlines, and get it done. Along the way, you are going to make hundreds of pivot moves, adjusting your ideas and/or concepts. This is all part of the learning curve.

All great ideas go through many changes and pivot moves to be successful. Thomas Edison and Henry Ford—probably the greatest visionaries on the planet—had many failures and made many pivot moves.

To become successful, the best advice I can give you, is not to listen too negative, boring, lazy people. If you do, you will want to quit every day. Be sure to stay positive and do your best work. Remember, every person you meet along the way of life has credentials that could help you. Be sure to keep an open mind and be *respectful*.

You may run into a person who wants to invest in your ideas, give you supplies, vehicles, etc. Treat everyone you meet with openness and kindness, and be approachable. The opportunity missed may be the missing link to putting your idea on the map to make millions. Just don't quit, and do not let any bitch, and/or person ever steal your dreams. Got it?

Lastly, do not take advise from losers, or people that know everything, but have never done anything. These fuckers, will wear you the fuck out. To spot these people, just look for the person whose lips are always moving and driving the junkiest car in the parking lot. This person is a fucking genius and is always broke, but they know everything. How the fuck can that person know everything, when they can't even pay their own bills?

39

Why Shopping With Women Is A Pain In The Ass

Shopping with women is a pain in the ass. They can never make up their minds about color, size or style. Finding clothes, household goods, automobiles—it's all confusing to women. If you as a guy, add your opinion to your girl's purchase, you will learn that it will take you twice as long and cost you more. Guys, trust me when I say, "Shut the fuck up". In the long run, being quiet will increase your chances of getting laid, and it will cost you less. Piss her off, and it will cost you twice as much, and no pussy. That was easy. Guys, did you learn something here?

This book makes life so easy, for we explain everything a man needs to know about shopping with a woman. When you're growing up, you never knew that everything with a woman is like negotiating a peace treaty with a foreign country. Get use to it, it ends on death you crazy bastards.

Now, that you are becoming an expert regarding women, you can go out and conquer the world. Good luck you little shit, you will need it. Always remember, if you want ass after shopping, to keep your mouth shut and just tell your lady what you think she wants to hear. That was easy. Don't fuck this up, or you get no booty tonight, you asshole. Got it.

40

Women Always Have To Have The Last Word

Women, always have to have the last word when it comes to an argument and/or disagreement. Remember when I told you about stupid conversations? Women, always have to put the last little dig into a conversation, just to light your fuse. You have heard enough stupid talk, and you thought it was over. Well, I am here to tell you, it's not over until the fat lady sings. Ha-ha.

Women, always have to get one more word in too ignite a conversation that makes no fucking sense, whatsoever. Holy shit, the bullshit never stops until death do us part. Ladies, let it go, it's going to be ok.

Think of the last disagreement you and your bitch got into? You knew it was going to be a losing battle, so you just shut the fuck up, and she just kept talking. It's truly amazing. Guys, let it go. Let them win, and move the fuck on. Remember, if she's still arguing with you, and you're not listening, your goal of getting laid is not going to happen. So, let her ramble on, if that is what makes her happy and makes her feel better. That's all you can do at this point. Got it.

THE END. It's over, bitch: you win. Your man has given up. We don't care anymore. We are tired. Can I still get laid tonight? WTF.

41

Women Hold Grudges Forever

Guys, I'm going to let you in on a secret. Women, hold grudges in the back of their little minds until death. That's right: women never forget shit. They never forget what you said, or what you did the whole time you're on the planet. Someone needs to teach them that the past is the past, and it's over, and they only need to worry about the future. That's all that matters anyway.

Sometimes, I think women are so miserable because they can't move forward without taking ten steps backward, or without remembering all the shit that happened in the past. Guys, when a situation comes up with your girl, that happened in the past, just ignore it. It is your best option. If you apologize again for it, you're a dick. If you argue about it, you're still a dick. If you continue to have conversations about it, you will always lose. Stop that shit today, its unhealthy.

Lastly, today's women for some reason gentlemen, cannot apologise when they are absolutely, fucking positively, wrong about something. They just can't do it, go figure. Men, be sure to apologise when you are in the wrong. Only apologise one time per situation, and then you are fucking done, got it.

So guys, listen to your girl's bullshit and keep your mouth shut. It's the only way to resolve these stupid conversations. This conversation is over, bitch. Let's move on with our lives. Holy shit; are you kidding me, what's next? Life goes on; ladies don't ruin life for all of us men, pretty please. Thank you.

42

You Have A 50/50 Shot Always To Get Booty

With marriage and dating, you have a 50/50 chance of getting laid each, and every day by your girl—if you play your cards right. Some guys are getting booty and some guys are not. That's why we call it "50/50". To increase your chances of getting laid daily, here are a few simple tips from, Colonel Smokes years of experience, that may help you. Get her flowers, bring home her favorite dessert, and buy her some pretty lingerie. By doing all this and getting her some nice gifts, you have a better chance of getting booty tonight. That was easy.

With women, it's emotional, whether or not they feel like giving you a piece of ass. It took men over 100 years to finally figure out what gets women in the mood to have sex: you spend days emotionally sucking up to your girl and telling her how pretty she is. You buy her gifts, you get her chocolates, and it still may not be good enough to get laid. Guys, the price of pussy can be very expensive, imagine that. Whatever you do, don't pay too much for a piece of ass. Some bitches even offer it for <u>free</u> I have heard, for Pete's Sake.

After 51 years of life and working my ass off, sometimes I don't have the energy for all that bullshit in order to get booty. Sometimes it's easier to just pay cash for it, and get a hooker that will service the account. Women don't understand this. Life is tough enough without having to beg for pussy.

You work hard at your job, you raise the family, you fix everything around the house, you mow the grass, you're tired—and now just to have sex, your woman wants to be romanced and caressed. Fuck that shit. I don't think so. I have cash and it works every time, bitch. Problem solved. So, Ladies, if your man is looking to get a piece of ass after a hard day of work, just give it to him without all your strings attached and everything will be just fine. By doing it this way, your man will always shop only at your store. That was easy.

The "Men's Romance Creed" for a hard-working American guy today, goes like this. Hi. How's your day? Do we need lube, tonight? That was fantastic. I am done. Goodnight and thank you. Now this, "Men's Romance Creed" shows his concern for you, tells you how wonderful you are in bed and thanks you for taking your valuable time out of your busy schedule to make your man happy. Problem solved, next. WTF.

This is sad, but this is all the energy a man can muster after putting up with all his woman's and families personal bull shit and working a fulltime job. Ladies, the day where a man has all kinds of time to romance you are simply gone. Remember, ladies, if you make it too hard for your man to get booty. He will just join the path of least resistance and go elsewhere.

Quit, trying to live some kind of fantasy life style with romance, you crazy bitch. It's all a dime a dozen and we both know that today. The fantasy ship has sailed, get over it. Remember, if you are married to it, it is part of your duties to take care of each other sexually. If you are just dating it, you have no obligation sexually to do anything.

One word of advice: never start any heavy discussions after dinner, or after 6 p.m. Always have them in the morning. Here is the reason: if you start a major discussion after dinner, you will always lose, and you will piss off your girl.

Getting laid is never going to happen. Just listen to her conversations, but have no opinion. If there is any chance of getting a piece of ass tonight, have very light conversation after 6 p.m. That time is the cut-off point to any heavy conversations. Tell her what you think she wants to hear, that always works.

By doing it this way, you have increased your chances of getting some booty by some 72.476 percent (estimated). If by now, you have had heavy conversation and have pissed her off, your 50/50 chance of getting laid just got squashed. You're fucked.

Gentlemen, women are like land mines: you never know when you've stepped on it, until they explode. Women, have hidden agendas and you will never know where their little minds are headed until you piss them off. Tread lightly and be sure to watch your step. When the land-mine goes off, you're fucked, get the hell out of there. Got it?

That was easy; remember nothing heavy after 6 pm. Don't ever forget the new rules. Colonel Smoke, (The Master) is always trying to help you get laid. Aren't you glad you now have the most powerful book regarding women. Look what you have learned so far? You are going to be a genius, just like all the women of the world.

43

Women's Questions Can Be Explosive

Men, do not answer these questions: *Do you like my shoes? Do you like my hair? Do you like my dress? Do you like my small boobs?* These are all loaded questions and have no right answers. If you say, "It looks fine," women read it as, you don't like it. If you say, "It's fantastic," they say you're lying. No matter what you say, it will always be interpreted the wrong way. WTF.

The funny thing is that the party and/ or gathering you're going to, is not about her. This is all a pain in the ass for men. Women need to relax and let their hair down, and just enjoy the moment. It's never good enough; they always want more and are never happy. Get over it, bitch. This party is not all about you; it's about going out and having fun with our friends, etc. Got it?

Ladies, we as men would love to answer your question. Just know that your man is trying hard to respond properly to you, so that you do not get offended and go off the deep end. If constructive criticism is not going to work for you, please don't ask us to comment on how you look if you are a sensitive person. Ladies, we are not here to sink our own ship with the ones we love. That's just plain stupid.

44

Social Media And Women:

Your girl and social media: this is the end of a normal woman. Social media, is too much information quickly for small minds, and it can destroy families. Women, get to see all their friends' new cars, their trips around the world, their new babies, and their new homes—and your woman thinks her life is shit because she has a new toaster. That's all fucked up.

So, remember, if your girl is on social media, Facebook, and/or Twitter all day, you will look like one big turd, because all her friends have everything and she has nothing, and you get her nothing. You are one, big, piece of shit in her eyes, even though you are doing all you can do.

Remember gentlemen, whatever you do, it's never going to be good enough when it comes to your women. Guys todays, American women want it all, and you are either a stepping stone for them to have it all, or you are the boulder that is in their fucking way. Kind of sad, but it is what it is. Got it.

Your girl's best friends, will always be your worst enemies; they're always trying to change and fix you. The problem is that you're not broken; they are. All women want to change, and/or mold their little man. Men, do not want to change. Leave us the fuck alone and we will be just fine. What the fuck? I give up.

Ladies, when it comes to social media, do it in moderation. Some people get so addicted to this shit that it will ruin and destroy their lives. Do not become a victim of this addictive habit. Take care of your family first, and if there is any time left over at the end of your day and you have taken care of your man, then go fuck with your social media. Get you priorities straight bitch, or your man is just going to leave and start shopping at a new store. The End.

If your relationship is already having troubles and you are trying to repair it, get the fuck off social media immediately. Facebook, twitter, Instagram and any of these other social networks are going to fuck up your life with the one that you love someday. I guarantee it, it's just a matter of time. 20 years ago, we did not have this stupid shit available to ruin a good relationship and yes ladies, you don't have to know everything, it's too much information for those little brains. You will go into overload, short circuit and go crazy. Men, this goes for you too, too much of any information can be overkill and destroy a good thing. Stop that shit immediately.

Don't wake-up and live for social media. It will destroy you, and eventually it will kill you and your family. Enough about social media.

45

Guys, Do Not Let Your Women Work For You

Women, need to work every day. It's healthy for women to work and generate revenue outside of the home. It gives their lives purpose and gets them out of bed every morning. Whatever you do, do not let the woman you sleep with work for you. It will fuck you up every time. I tried this, and it does not work, even if you set up all the ground rules ahead of time. Eventually, you will get screwed.

Self-employment, is another area most women don't seem to understand. Self-employment is the hardest thing an individual can do to support his family. Self-employment consist of always trying to provide a living to support you, your family and your employees. You have to hire employees, manage employees, buy supplies, purchase insurance, get workman's comp, unemployment issues, liability problems, vehicles and maintance, equipment, phones, sales, health insurance, contracts, purchase orders, legal issues, attorney related issues, vehicle wrecks, fights in office, permits, licenses, manage receivables, hire accountants, debts, conflicts, rent, building maintance, a/c, computers, internet, salary negotiating. This is just the tip of the ice berg. It never fucking stops.

Being self-employment is the biggest pain is the ass, but it could have some really nice benefits, or it could bankrupt you and your family. Ladies, if you have not been self-employed over the last five years, please do not tell your little man he is doing everything all wrong.

If your man is self-employed, support him the best you can, and listen to him if he is in a bad mood. Be nice to him if he is exhausted, and just be their instead of telling him what he is doing is always wrong. Self-employment that makes real money, is the hardest employment that any person could ever do. Most women for some reason, don't seem to understand that, why, because us men make it look so easy. Trust me, it's not easy at all, it's a bitch.

Remember men, if your girl is self-employed and you are not, just support her the best way you can. It works both ways. Self-employment, now that you understand it, is the hardest thing you will ever do in your adult business life. Working for someone might be tough, but in no way is it as tough as self-employment. Self-employment, as you can see, is much more than managing employees, it's about signing your name to your employees pay checks every week and praying that the checks won't bounce, and that you have enough money in the account to cover your expenses. Managing people is easy compared to paying and writing the checks to employees every week. Good luck in your business. I hope your partner has learned something from this book that will make them more supportive to you every day.

Most men try to give more time and money to their family members than they had growing up. I understand your kindness in trying to help your family, but don't go overboard taking care of someone in your family, for it could bankrupt you. I see this all the time. Your help is not appreciated as much as you might think it is with this new generation, I promise. So, be sure to take care of yourself first, for if your health goes down, you are no good to anyone.

Last but not least, when it comes to dealing with business, don't give your opinion unless its requested. Don't give any advice. Nobody wants to hear your opinion or take your advice in today's world anyway. Everyone today is a fucking genius. Let it GO.

Don't hold grudges and be sure to listen twice as much as you talk. Remember, as the boss of a business, your rules and guide lines don't mean shit to most of today's employees. Just be the boss and do the best you can. In a couple of years all employees will be replaced with robots anyway, and that will solve all your employee issues with women and men. Ha-ha. That was easy.

Your women will change, and/or fuck up all your rules that you have created anyway for your business. After a short period of time, women working for you, will know your job better than you; they will give you all this advice to make your business work better, go faster, and increase production. The problem with this is that you have already tried this shit and it does not work. Try explaining this to some bitch who thinks she is a genius, and knows more about your business than you do. That would be a stupid conversation that you could never win. Don't do it, fellows. You will lose every time, and you will get no booty for a month. Do you understand?

Lastly, gentlemen, I want to explain communication; texting, emailing, Facebook, social media, and sending pictures throughout the day to your special person is stupid. Doing this will only sink your own ship. Let me explain. These tools should only be used exclusively for business during business hours. Using it personally throughout the day, you are going to say or do something your lady will not like.

It will get miss construed, it will be interpreted the wrong way, taken out of context, and/or a picture will be taken with the wrong people in it, and piss her off. Something you did will get fucked up and then your day is shot.

When you are super busy trying to run your business to make a profit, it is very easy to send the wrong shit, to the wrong place, at the wrong time. Stop that shit today, just text "hi" twice a day with your phone to your special lady. That's it, this lets her know you are alive and kicking, problem solved.

Ladies, same goes for you. Don't text, email, or Facebook your man all day long. He is very busy. There are only 24 hours in a day for him to try to make a living, you blowing up his phone for stupid shit is a big distraction throughout the day. Please stop immediately so that he can try to make enough money throughout the day, so you can keep the roof over your family's head.

Also, gentlemen, your computer and your telephone are off limits to your bitch. Do not let your girl go on your personal computer, or borrow your phone. Men, are not always guilty, but the bull shit that can happen when she gets on your computer and or/your phone is endless. Don't do it. Nothing good can ever come from this, and your settings and passwords will get all fucked up, too. Don't let her do it, you asshole, unless it's an emergency. Guys, this goes for you to; Stay off all of her shit. Got it. The End.

When it comes to running a business, hire the best people you can find. Family most of the time will not work. They will be disrespectful to you, and be ungrateful for all the things you try to do for them. Got it. This is a lot to learn, I know.

46

Women Will Never Understand Cause And Effect

One thing women will never understand is cause and effect. It works like this: I tell my little child Johnny to mow the yard today. I come home from work, and the grass in the yard is still a foot tall. I ask my girl why the yard is not mowed. She answers, "Little Johnny forgot". I blow a gasket and tell the little fuck stick to mow the grass, now. He smarts off and says, no. I scream and tell the little fuck to mow it now. This raising of the voice is called narcissism in America, but it really is not. It's called "little piece-of-shit Johnny is being disrespectful."

So, because I asked that little fuck stick to mow the grass and he refuses to, my life that night is shit. My girl is pissed off at me. My dinner is cold; no one talks at the dinner table. I supposedly am an asshole, and I don't get laid because Johnny did not mow the grass. How's the fuck does that shit work? I worked all day to pay the bills, keep the cars running, and buy food, but in the end, I'm a fucking piece of shit. This is what cause and effect is, and women don't seem to understand it.

Holy shit, you can only explain shit so many times in one's lifetime. What the fuck? It never ends. Johnny, mow the fucking grass, please! Thank you. Now that is not being disrespectful.

47

Women Can't Understand Normal Thinking

Women, Can't Understand Normal Thinking because of their emotional nonsense. When you combine emotional thinking with no logic or facts, you are going to get a stupid answer. Emotions have no place in business for making good decisions.

All great decisions are based on reality and factual thinking. I can't tell you how many times I have put a question to a female, and she put her emotions into a question that could be resolved in minutes. Because of emotional nonsense, it takes fucking days. Women, complicate easy problems. Now, because of bad decisions and no logic, the situation implodes into a cluster fuck on steroids.

Remember, to always rent it, so that way if it gets stupid, you can always trade it in and get a new sexier model. Women, can be like old cars when they get all fucked up, they become very expensive to repair, they are always breaking down, and they are always at the mechanics' shop trying to be fixed.

Moral of the story; always drive a young, clean, and sexy version and all your problems are solved. Ha. That was easy, NOT. Remember guys, this shit with women never stops until death. Got it.

48

Why Do Girls Act Like Their Mothers?

Look at your girl's mother. Is she nice? Is she pretty? Is she a bitch? Is she nasty? I'm here to tell you that your girl's mother is going to be what your girl acts and looks like over time. If you don't like your girl's mother, run fast. Ninety percent (estimated) of the time, your girl will be just like her mother. Don't put too much emphasis on the girl's father; for he was just the sperm donor to that unit. He worked hard, played hard, and put up with a lot of shit from those fucked up women.

Sometimes, the father of the girl will flat out tell you that his daughter is very special and caring, or that she is a pain in the ass and to stay away from her. Fathers tell it like it is. Talk to the father. He knows, trust me. Look at all the valuable information that you can get for free from her father.

But, if the father is tired of his daughter's bullshit and wants her out of the house, he may lie to you just to get her married off. So be very careful, and listen intently; that way you won't get caught up in this scam. Wow, this is a lot of confusing information for a little boy who just wants to tap some ass. Now, do you understand why we rent? That was easy.

49

Child Support And Alimony

Guys, this is some serious shit. Child support is exactly what it says it is. You get to support a child until he becomes an adult, and/or finishes college, and/or earns a degree, what the fuck, they never told me that. The average child today costs more than $ 1 million U.S. dollars (estimated) to raise from an infant to a college graduate. Guys, some children don't graduate from college till they are 35 years old. Holy Shit.

The birth of a new child today in America costs more than $50,000. The doctors, the hospitals, the anesthesiologists, the nurses—it's unbelievable, that's if there are no complications. So my advice is this: if you hear the phrase, "child support," run like hell, because you will get fucked. It's never going to be fair, trust me.

Women, only care that you pay your monthly child support and you may never get to see your child. A monthly child support payment of $2,500 and up, is not unheard of today. Guys, it's fucking expensive. Fuck that shit. Get a dog.

Always have protection and a good raincoat to prevent this shit from happening. Women use children as pawns. As you just learned, child support does not stop in some states until the child decides to finish college. Some of these little pain-in-the-asses may never finish. On a serious note, child support is not funny and it's very expensive, but if you agreed to it, pay for it at all cost, for it is your child.

Alimony, is another scam that women are experts on, or become experts on after marriage when getting divorced. You get to pay some bitch—who you can't stand—for the rest of your adult life, until death. Now that's fucked up. Can you imagine signing a contract to give $10,000 monthly to someone who you can't stand or hate? Welcome to alimony.

This is called alimony, and it is buried in all marriage licenses somewhere when you try to dissolve them in America. This is a goat fucking. This is what a marriage license is. It is a legal instrument that will fuck you for the rest of your adult life when you try to get rid of the license. Who the hell would ever sign a contract that has no end date in sight, except death? That's fucked up.

If you would have known this before marriage, do you think you would have ever gotten married? All you were trying to do, was to get laid. Makes you think twice about marriage.

If you have learned anything from this book, just rent the booty and then you will only pay for what you use. Why pay for something all your life, that you don't get to use for ever, (alimony). Rent it. Now that makes sense. Do you understand? I have room to explain more if I need to.

There are guys out there who pay 50% of their net salary to some bitch who they cannot stand. Don't let one of them be you. Remember, if that crazy bitch somehow dies, the alimony stops. That's interesting; it just makes you think. Okay, enough said.

50

Women And Money

Most women, can't stop spending money. It's not in their DNA. They spend money on clothes, kids, hair products, spa treatments, etc. It never ends when it comes to women and money. Guys, you must put women on a budget to control this crazy, fucked up behavior. Spending money that you don't have will bankrupt you, ruin relationships, and destroy your family. Holy shit.

Alcohol addiction and drug addiction are no different from a spending addiction. They destroy everything you worked for your whole life. Guys, women don't like it when you put them on a budget. Gentlemen, women think money grows on trees. They spend money like its water, free flowing and endless. Guys, never combine checking, savings accounts with your significant other. It does not work.

In the past with the old generation it might have worked to co-mingle funds, but today that would be an absolute disaster. Don't do it, your account will get overdrawn, checks will bounce, it will get all fucked up, yet it still all your fault and you had nothing to do with it. Go figure.

All individuals should have their own checking accounts, savings accounts, credit cards, and then there is no confusion when it gets all fucked up. If you want to have one checking account for your family that you share, then this is fine. All accounts must be separate, so that way you are never denied pussy over money that was spent on shit that you did not know about.

We as guys, can only work so hard and do so much to fix their spending problems. If you can be successful and get your girl's spending money under control, then you have a chance to make it with your bitch. That was easy.

I am not a big believer of comingling funds or having joint accounts with your female. This just creates more arguments. You must watch all credit card bills, and checking accounts, and give a weekly allotment for spending. This is probably considered narcissistic to women, but these crazy bitches don't get it until you set the limits on spending.

If you have unlimited funds and make millions of dollars, then this will not apply to you. But if you are like 99% of the rest of us, broke dead fucks (BDF) in the world, then get your budget under control today. Makes sense, right?

Women think, money grows on trees. Women think that if they have a check book, it must have money in it. Ha-ha. If women have a credit card in their purse, they think it is an open invitation to spend money. Ninety-eight percent of most arguments between men and women, are all about money and booty. If you want to start an unintelligent, stupid conversation with your woman, start talking about interest rates, leverage, debt and credit. Now, you fucked up. You will never win that battle.

Women, always play possum and act stupid when it comes to money. I don't know if they really are stupid, or are just playing their normal cat-and-mouse games. Ladies, I am here to tell you two things: one, the credit cards are for emergencies only. Do not put any purchases on the credit card unless it's an emergency. Two, do not spend money in the check book that you (or we) do not have. It's that simple. Get it? Stop the spending nonsense, you crazy bitch. You are wearing my ass out. Enough said.

51

Love, Sex, And Rape

Women, sometimes confuse love, sex, and rape. This can become complicated when you get all the female emotions involved. Women think differently from men. Men, only care about getting booty, with little respect given to long-term feelings. Women, read into everything you say and do. Guys, are looking to get laid, have sex, and that's it. When meeting women, we as men don't get attached; we just want to test drive. We are like car shoppers. We test drive until we find something that we like. Women, on the other hand, think every time they sleep with a guy that it is all about love. That's bullshit. This is called sex for us guys, and we both had a little piece of enjoyment. That's it. On a serious note, always wear a condom when the monkey is playing. The rule of thought here gentlemen, is the four W's: wrap it up, wiggle it in, wiggle it out, and wash it off since you never know where that female unit has been parked all this time. Got it? Enough said.

Love for a guy, is when he sleeps with a female and continues to spend time with her, starts to have feelings for her, and does not want to spend time with anyone else. Women don't understand that men fall in love with women 2% (estimated) of the time when they sleep with them. So, ladies, enjoy all your free dinners, free movies, free outings, and always be grateful for what your male friend does for you. Be sure to put out when you need to. Remember, the gentlemen's motto revolves around the five F's when we are looking for a lay. Find them, feel them, fuck them, have fun with them, and forget them. That was easy. Women who are nasty and mean qualify for the five F's program only. Got it? Do you understand? Enough said.

Most guys don't rape women. Some women get confused when they have had consensual sex with a male and the outcome was not what they wanted. Both the female and the male had some drinks, did some drugs, got drunk, and screwed each other's brains out. The next morning the girl is not feeling too good about herself. She wakes up pregnant, she got STDs, and she is aggravated because the man did not stay for breakfast. WTF.

Anyway, women start putting emotional thought into what they did, and they are not proud of it. Instead of blaming themselves for their party-like sex rendezvous, they call it rape, and want to punish whoever they can. This is such bullshit. Only truly sick, fucked up women, will pull this shit. Don't become a victim of some crazy, fucked up, chemically imbalanced bitch. This is fucked up as a football bat. Get it? It makes no sense. Remember ladies, if you are a willing participant in having sex, it's not called rape when you're done. It's called sex, and you should have enjoyed the wild ride. That was easy.

Also, guys remember, that any female younger than eighteen years old is not considered an adult. She does not have the legal ability to say yes to have sex. Do not go there. Remember, older women can take advantage of underage males and this is called rape, too. I hate it when that shit happens. For some reason, when boys get violated by a woman, it's not a big deal; but watch out when a woman who's less than 18 years of age gets violated. Someone is going to jail. That's fucked up.

Women, it's not rape just because you woke up and you feel bad about yourself. What the fuck? Get a life, bitch. You make me tired and where my ass out. Gentlemen, always respect the ladies. Remember ladies, when we guys say you look very pretty today, this is not sexual harassment. We are trying to be nice. Today's women, get so confused and always want to sue your ass for just being nice. Go figure. WTF. As a guy, you always be on the short end of the stick.

52

Why All Women Should Work Outside The Home

It's a good thing if your female is employed outside the home. Working outside the home is good for building self-esteem, finding new friends, and challenging her mental abilities. I have always believed that it's healthy to have something to get out of bed for and to accomplish a task.

Another good thing about your bitch working outside the home, is that she can't spend any money when she is working on her employer's clock. So, if your significant other is employed, you're saving in two ways. She's making money, and she can't spend your money at the same time. Well, some women can do both, I guess. Got to love Amazon.

Also, by having your woman work outside of the home, she now knows the value of a dollar. Remember ladies, money does not grow on trees, so get to work you crazy bitch. Ha-ha, that was a joke. Guys don't try saying this shit at home; it will not go over too well with your woman.

If you say too much, your female may try to cut off the pussy and you may have to sleep in the other room, or you could just go find a new piece of ass. That was easy. Men, always take the path of least resistance, ladies don't ever forget that. Quit making it so hard on us! What's the next problem?

53

Life Partner? Never Thought Of That

In the end, if your girl insists on having a commitment (being married), and she does not qualify for marriage under our new rules on net worth, a life partnership may be the answer. A life partnership is another excellent way to be committed to your bitch.

Some states recognize a life partnership as equal to a marriage, with all the same rights and benefits as a marriage license. With a life partnership, you can file joint income tax returns, and receive health insurance and government benefits together. Check with your state to see if you qualify.

The nicest thing about a life partnership, if your state has one, is that if you separate, you just notify the state by filling out the state's paperwork signifying that your life partnership has ended—no alimony or financial benefits to get tied up in a legal mess. The genius who thought of this deserves a fucking medal.

54

All Pussy Has A Price

Gentlemen, all pussy has a price and you're going to pay for it one way or another. Women know this and we guys are slow, but we have just figured this out, too. Giving gifts, flowers, and jewelry, and buying dinners are all part of the expensive cost of dating and finding the right lady for you. It gets very expensive when you are out with a girl who you can't stand. The cost, and/or price of expenses differ depending on how much you like the person. Regardless, you're going to pay something to get laid. Got it? Guys, it is not free and all women know it.

Look at women as a toll road: the more you drive on that road, the more it costs. The cool thing about renting is that when you get tired of paying and the road becomes bumpy, or has a pothole, you can always get off at the next exit and get on another road. Women, men know up front that all pussy has a price. We get it now. Lots of times we are trying to figure out if the price of your toll road is worth the joy and happiness it might bring us. Women, seem to forget all the good shit that men do for them. So, for that reason, we are always looking at the price of the tolls, and comparing it to the amount of joy you might bring us. That was easy. Ladies, when we bring you flowers, take you out to dinner, and/or buy you a gift, don't turn into a nagging bitch. Control your emotions, take your fucking medicine and be grateful for what you have. Women, don't forget that you all have jobs today, too. You have college degrees. You're smarter than anyone on the planet, you know everything and you are all geniuses. You can treat your man and take him out for dinner, and give him nice gifts, too. In today's world, it's called a two-way street, bitch. Get it? So now ladies, we equal.

55

Men Are Tired Of Flowers And Jewelry

Women, love it when you give them flowers and jewelry. Most men know that when you give a gift to a female, it means you care for her. Remember ladies, it's the thought that counts. I have over the years given gifts to females and they have not liked the color, the design, the layout, or it was not expensive enough. Women, the best words of advice that I can give you are the following: Shut the fuck up and just say, "Thank you". It does not matter if you don't like it. He gave you a gift and he bought it for you. That should count for something.

Some ladies with their nasty attitudes, forget that this is when you're supposed to appreciate what your guy does for you, and say, thank you, "Hello." Nice words are so easy to say, but for some reason most women and men today can't say them correctly. Next time someone does something nice for you; go out of your way to thank them. That was easy, you now feel better.

Guys, are over these nasty, conniving, self-centered bitches. Guys don't want to buy gifts for anyone anymore, for they're tired of all this ungratefulness. Some women don't know how to be thankful. What the fuck? So remember, ladies: next time your man gives you a gift, just pretend to like it and say, "Thank you". It's so fucking simple. That was easy. Do you understand? Can I be more clear? Always remember, it's the thought that counts, you nut.

56

Unintelligent, Stupid Conversations

Women, like to twist conversations. Have you ever had a conversation and explained everything correctly to a woman, and it comes back reversed, twisted, stupid, and just outright ignorant?

How do you stop stupid, twisted stories from happening? You can't; just go along with it. The more you try to straighten out stupid shit, the more you're an asshole. Forget it, keep your mouth shut, and just listen. Eventually it will end, and a new day will begin. Thank God for that.

Conversations that have no right answers to women, will not work. This goes on with relationships till the day women die. Women want to discuss shit that will not work or can't be done. It's called "stupid conversation," and it's a total waste of your time and money. Have you ever had a conversation that was absolutely stupid? Well, I'm here to tell you that the only thing you can do is either listen, keep your mouth shut, or divert the topic.

When I was growing up, I learned this from my mother. If I did something wrong, or my mother did not like my behavior, she would divert my attention to something else that would change my behavior. It worked, until I figured out what my mom was doing.

Guys, I am here to tell you: do not engage in unintelligent, stupid conversation with your girl. Don't argue with your lady about shit that does not matter. You will never win. It will never make sense, and it's a total waste of time. "Keep your mouth shut," is the only answer. You can't win an argument with stupid. Do you get it? Do you need me to re-explain?

Guys, whatever you do, do not act, or talk stupid to your girl, either. From time to time, you will want to indulge in conversation with your girl to fix things. It will make you look like a real asshole. Shut the fuck up if you don't have something intelligent to say. Enough about stupid conversations.

57

When Keeping Your Mouth Shut Will Not Work

If keeping your mouth shut will not work, and you must give an answer to a stupid question that makes no sense, then just answer with one of these: "Oh, okay," or "That's, ah, interesting," or "Hmmm". By using one of these, you act like you care, but in reality, who gives a shit? The question is stupid and makes no sense.

A stupid conversation about shit that has no right answer is a favorite pastime for women who have too much time on their hands. Get a job, bitch. What the fuck?

58

Prenuptial Agreements Are A Must

Prenuptial agreements, are contracts that are created to be litigated if you ever get divorced. If you must get married, definitely get a prenuptial agreement. We have included a prenuptial agreement in the back of this book for your convenience. It is a short one, that is made to be funny and entertaining, but gives you an idea. Always consult with your scamming attorney if you are in need of a prenuptial agreement.

If you plan on having a net worth of zero, you may not need a prenuptial agreement. Prenuptial agreements are supposed to protect the assets that you have acquired before marriage, and beyond. They do not always work in this fucked up, litigious society, here in America.

If you ever need your prenuptial agreement because you fell out of love with your woman, the scamming attorneys will work on ripping this agreement apart, and explaining how it was not fair prior to you getting married. Trust me when I say, prenuptial agreements are another joke of our fucked up legal system.

A better way might be to get a gun. Then you can explain, discuss, and reinforce your written, legal, prenuptial agreement with the scamming, douche bag attorneys. Sometimes these piece of shit attorneys understand things quicker this way. Attorneys, are not totally stupid and do possess a little bit of common sense when it comes to guns. Most attorneys do not want to get shot, for they all have families, too.

If a big stud attorney sees that you carry a gun, he or she most likely won't scam you, or try to manipulate the legal verbiage in your prenuptial agreement. Attorneys, are not fucking stupid.

People of the state of Texas understand this shit all too well, and so do most of their wonderful attorneys. Attorneys, will not scam you if they understand they will be held accountable for their actions. Always carry your gun when dealing with attorneys. Moral of the story here, Mr. or Mrs. Wonderful, Genius, Fantastic Attorney, is don't fuck with any of my financial agreements, or be prepared to pay for it with your own life. Do you understand? Case closed. That was easy. THE END. No refunds here. Anything else. Are you clear, you assholes?

59

Find A Girl Like Your Mother

Guys, the days of finding a girl like your mother are over. Women of today, do not want to cook, they don't want to clean the house, and they damn sure don't want to do laundry. It's all about them, equal rights and equal pay. It's all bullshit. Guys, women are all geniuses today if you did not already know.

Men, on the other hand, are only here on the planet to be slaves to the women of the world. Now that is fucked up. Men, grow some balls and quit acting like a pussy.

Who the hell gave these bitches the rights to vote and drive? What the fuck were they thinking? Women of today, know everything. Guys, get used to it: the days of women cleaning the house, and staying home to take care of the family and their man, are long gone. You, as a guy, need to ask yourself if the price of pussy is worth the aggravation and expense? I personally don't think so. Rent everything.

After my divorce, I figured the price of pussy cost over $1,100 per piece of ass, estimated on my divorce settlement. Blow jobs were off the charts at $1,500,000 apiece, estimated.

That's some expensive shit. A good hooker does not make this salary, and you are paying for her to leave, anyway. That's why they always leave. I am here to tell you that there is a cost for booty and as long as you are renting it, it might be worth it. That was easy.

Getting married to a female today could punish you for the rest of your adult life, and it can be financial suicide until death. The leverage and control one gets through a marriage contract is bullshit. Ask any one of your friends who is still financially sound after his divorce, if he would ever get married again? His response will be, "Hell, no, fuck that shit". After paying the attorneys, mediators, forensic auditors, counselors, witnesses and every other professional—are you fucking kidding me? You would have to be crazy, but some men still do it.

I think we all know the answer to the question "Marriage contract or hooker"? sounds pretty reasonable. Rent it. No marriage contracts needed here. Do you understand yet? Are you learning something here?

60

Quality Of Women Is Down A Little In The Twenty-First Century

The quality of a good old Southern woman who is morally grounded, who can cook, clean your home, take care of her man, raise the children, and not be a pill popper is less than 1%. Good luck finding that shit.

Women of today, are all high maintenance, and they all come with a bag of bullshit. Their families are all fucked up, they drink too much, they have screwed up kids, they've got bills, their employment is all fucked up, and if you choose to marry her, it is now your job to fix all that shit. It will never happen, but men kill themselves trying. Rent that shit. Do you understand yet?

If men had one wish to be granted by women, the wish would be for women to stop all of the female drama. I don't know why this is, but women love drama. They love to be around it, love to create it, and love to see it in action.

Drama, comes in many forms. It could be drama talk regarding their health, employment, car, family, kids, school, or possibly their relationship with a male. Holy shit! Women can create drama when they're sound asleep, for Pete's sake.

The moral of the story gentlemen, is that you will need to learn how to handle this crazy shit. I personally deal with drama by ignoring it, pretending I don't hear it, and hoping it will go away.

I also use diversion and try to change the subject matter of the drama. No matter how you deal with it, your girl will have it, and it never goes away.

Ladies, if you're listening, stop with all that crazy drama. We, as men, have to put up with so much shit every day that we have zero tolerance for all this unwanted and unnecessary drama. So if you are a drama queen, go back to your castle, lock the fucking door, and throw away the key, please. Do you understand?

Ladies, we men are tired of all your fucking drama and don't want to hear it anymore. Get the hell out. Drama class is over, you all passed with flying colors. Stop that shit, immediately. THE END.

60.5

Women Don't Like Constructive Criticism?

Constructive criticism, is part of the learning and educational process. American women of today, know everything about everything. You can't tell women anything without them getting their panties all twisted and wotted up. This catty bullshit is a new trait that we have allowed women to do with the American women's lib movement. This is totally fucking unacceptable.

Men, grow some balls, please. All American men know today that the whole world revolves around what women want, and the power of the pussy. Ladies of America today, are all geniuses. We men get it. Done. Ladies, you WIN. Fight is over. We men are exhausted. We have thrown up the white flag.

Now that we men, have finally figured out women, we are putting all women on notice how to handle constructive criticism, or constructive communication (also known as learning and education) ……. You women do not know everything, even though you think you all do. Next time your asshole man explains something of importance, or tries to help, and/or support your ass, DO NOT TURN INTO A NASTY, MISERABLE, CRAZY BITCH! We are tired of that shit. Be fucking nice. Got it.

Women reverse course, and go off in the wrong direction all the time when having adult conversations. I can't tell you how many times men have tried to have some simple communication with a woman, and the bitch blows it all up (starts screaming), and creates an issue that never even existed. What the fuck is that all about? Control those raging hormones, please. Always take your medication if your Doctor has prescribed it. We guys all know what happens when you forget to take your hormone medicine, and/or birth control pills. Holy shit, watch the fuck out. We don't need the cops here tonight, bitch.

From here on out, ladies listen to your man intensely, don't mouth off, and don't fly off the handle and go crazy every time you communicate with your man. Guys, same goes for you. If your girl has some constructive criticism, then just follow the instructions you have just learned above, and everything will be just fine.

Ladies, when men think your constructive criticism or communication is stupid or wrong, we just shut up and ignore you and walk away. We don't go crazy. Hopefully, women have learned something from this chapter and understand that they do not always have to be right. You don't have to argue about every dam thing that we try to help you with.

Men, already know if we did not have an attached penis to our bodies, you women would not need us for anything. We get it. Its Ok. The moral of the story, is always be kind, nice and respectful, and everything will be just fine. That was easy. What's the next problem!

Part II
LIFE SKILLS

61

People Are A Pain In The Ass. Why?

You can influence people, but you can't change their bad behavior, disrespect, ungratefulness, etc. When I was 18, I thought I could help and educate stupid people. I have learned over the years that many people are just plain crooked. They scam, lie, cheat and just do bad things to one another. It's very sad, but its life in the 21st Century.

Family, is probably the worst when it comes to unbelievable behavior against one another. Today's generation (millennials), think they are owed everything, and that they are above the rest. That's just fucked up. These pieces of shit are disrespectful, ungrateful and just unappreciative. Go figure.

When it comes to family and friends, do not loan them any money, it will burn you every time. You should give money as a gift, only if you have it to give. Do not get in business with family members. You will always get screwed, and/or they will tell the world that you screwed them. Do not loan vehicles, jet skis, chainsaws, or any other material items unless you want to give them as gifts. They will ruin or lose them.

Remember, when you have assets, loaning items creates a major liability for you and your family if they have an accident. Again, this is why it does not pay to own anything that you're going to loan out. Rent it all. That was easy.

62

Forgive Everyone

As a 51-year-old person, I can say I can forgive anyone who rips me off, steals from me, disrespects me, or is ungrateful towards me. It's harder to forgive people when you're younger, but as time goes on, you realize that the only one who hurts by not forgiving them is yourself. Holding grudges and being angry in this short time we are here on this planet is a total waste of time, and is unhealthy. Life is short. Enjoy every day, influence whoever you can, and become the best person you can be.

If you claim to be religious, and follow the lord, it's not just a part-time job. Going to church on Sundays, and asking for forgiveness for all the scamming bull shit you did Monday through Saturday is not how GOD intended for you to behave. Some of you go to church, and are sweet, kind, and loveable on Sundays, and then turn into total pieces of shit for the rest of the week. You scam everyone, you don't pay your bills, you are rude, you are selfish and obnoxious. That's just plain wrong.

Being religious and following the lord is a full-time job. Stop being fake. Your religious behavior should reflect that Monday through Sunday, not just on Sundays.

So, if you truly are a religious person, quit being a piece of shit six days a week and asking for forgiveness on Sunday, the seventh day. You scamming religious people know all the nasty, lying, cheating bull shit you did to others during the week, and that in the "Eyes of the Lord" is not good and you might even go to hell for that evil behavior. Stop that shit immediately, if you truly are claiming to be a full-time religious person.

You look really bad in front of others when you are a two timer, religious, scamming piece of shit. Always take the high road when it comes to religion, you will be glad you did. Remember, always treat people the way you would want to be treated. The End.

Somewhere in the Bible it says, "forgive those who trespass against us". I can truly say that Colonel Smoke, the author of this book, has not read the Bible from cover to cover, but he understands you have to have forgiveness in your heart to live amongst these assholes. I do believe that if you don't forgive everyone that screws you, or rips you off, you will be one miserable person and a pain in the ass to the people you love. If you don't forgive people, no matter what people have done to you, the only one you are hurting is yourself. That's it, plain and simple.

The world is full of thieves, liars and cheats. If you find two friends in your lifetime that you can trust to the ends of the earth, you have more than 99% of the rest of the people around you. Count your blessings and your friends every day, you will be able to do it on one hand. They are precious, and they are only here on this earth for a limited time. Call or text them every day, and tell them how much you truly love them.

63

Broke People Are Lousy Advisors

When getting advice from broke folks who know everything, be careful. Some people you will meet during your life span will know everything about everything and are dead broke, but are geniuses. Huh. I have found that these BDFs—Broke Dead Fucks—just want to talk about how great they are. Throughout life, your job is to stay clear from these BDFs. They have little to teach you, and they can suck the life and money right out of you.

Remember, when you need information about life, business or employment, ask people who have had experiences or challenges, similar to the ones you've had. These people can be really helpful sometimes in sharing what did, or did not work in their situations.

Successful business owners, that are running businesses today are the most knowledgeable people when it comes to getting advice. They have seen it all. They have pain-in-the-ass employees, they have had shit stolen, they have had Internal Revenue Service situations, and they are just well-rounded individuals.

Business owners, that were running businesses years ago, I have learned, have no clue how things work today. They just like to talk and ramble about how great they were, but they don't understand "the new world", of how business is done. Shake hands with them, smile at them, be polite to them, and tell them to have a glorious, fantastic wonderful day for they have no clue. The End.

Ask any *successful* business owner, running a business today, any questions about business, and I am sure he or she can help you with your situation. Moral of the story is this: get advice only from people who truly are qualified to give it. These people are successful, and already understand how business is done. That was easy.

64

Attorneys Are All Crooks, And All Agreements Are Designed To Be Litigated

Paperwork, contracts, and agreements are all written to bring on litigation today. If one party of a contract is honorable, and the other party is a scammer, then the honorable party will always get fucked. Case in point: the scammer only signs contracts to gain leverage to money or products to screw somebody. He or she probably had no plans to pay for it, and fulfill their obligation anyway. Don't do business with crooks or scammers; you will always get screwed. Shoot these fuckers.

Always Google any businessperson you want to do business with, and find out if they've done any unscrupulous, and/or unethical activities. When doing business, or purchasing a product, you should not always take the lowest price. The cheapest price will most always fuck you. Always try to get a referral from a business, and/or an individual, if you plan on hiring someone.

Lawyers, love to litigate everything; that is how they scam and make money. They will litigate anything for any reason, with no cause, just to scam you out of your money here in America. When all your assets and money are gone, your attorney will disappear quickly. Lawyers love paperwork, love to review it, and love to fuck it all up, so they can review it again and again. It's called the, "billable hour scam" and now we all know about it.

I'm always amazed that lawyers don't get shot for fucking all these innocent people with their fucking scams. If I had a bad kidney, or I was terminally ill, and got fucked by some piece of shit attorney, I would shoot that scamming, "piece of shit" right between the eye balls. No Questions asked, problem solved. Moral of the story, if you are going to be a law-abiding attorney, don't be a scamming piece of shit. Remember, you scamming piece of shit attorneys, you only get to fuck the one person wrong, one time and then you're dead. The lesson here, Mr. or Mrs. Wonderful, Fantastic, Know-It-All Attorney, is to be very careful who you decide to fuck over, for it could be your last time. Got it?

If you are a scamming piece of shit attorney, I hope you understand lead poisoning. Lead poisoning is a new disease that you, an attorney can catch, when you scam an honest individual and are wasting their time and money in court defending themselves on shit that is total bullshit. You created this scam for your own financial gain, with no real cause with the honorable party. The legal term for this is called, "fucking an honorable party without cause". Bet you never heard of that. Not good, I would not be too proud of this.

With lead poisoning, the honorable party then takes his weapon of choice, and shoots the scamming attorney between the eye balls, so the scamming attorney will never fuck any honest person or business ever again. This is called lead poisoning. Do you, asshole attorney, understand that lead poisoning this way, is a one-page, simple, unilateral contract, that works every time with a non-refundable deposit just like you fucker's charge? You should be able to understand that. Put that in your pipe and smoke it, you asshole. Next time you are walking to your car, and/or enjoying your family, be sure you are careful if you are one of these douche bag attorneys that has fucked somebody, for you could have fucked over the one person with the bad kidney, and end up catching, the new lead poisoning disease. Your family might miss you!

This person will probable change your attitude from one cocky fuck attorney, to something quite different if you survive. Good fucking luck, if you are one of these asshole, scamming, piece of shit attorneys. If you are a productive, valuable, legal member of our society, then you should have nothing to worry about. Makes you think who you really are, and if you are considered a good person or not. Just a thought, be very careful.

Remember, to always carry your gun if you must deal with attorneys. By doing this, everyone understands that you are here to get things done properly. Enough said. By getting rid of some of these scumbag attorneys, we might be able to clean up our fucked up legal system. Today, most products are not made in the United States of America, because of all the liability lawsuits that these wonderful, amazing, law-abiding, douche bag lawyers have concocted. It's all fucked up today.

Getting a judgment against someone who has screwed you is mostly a waste of time and money. Ninety-five percent (estimated) of all judgments are not collectable. They cost a fortune to get, and very rarely get paid out. Now, if you get a judgment against an insurance company or the government, it may be better than hitting the lottery. Don't hold your breath.

In short, if you must sue someone, all attorneys will tell you, that you will prevail and get rich so that they can get your up-front money and/or retainer. If they told you that you had no case and to save your money, they would make nothing, but they never say that. Fuck those attorneys. They are all a bunch of crooks anyway. Suing takes years, and it takes years off your life. If you are over 50, don't spend the rest of your good years fucking around with attorneys, investigators, and judges. In the end, they will always fuck you anyway. Does it really matter? I don't think so, enjoy life every day.

65

Bankruptcy, Scams, And Cheats: Does Anybody Pay Their Bills Anymore?

Today's world, is much different than it was 20 years ago, when people had honor and morals in paying their bills and obligations. You used to be able to do business on a handshake; you would never think of doing this today. Today's businesses and individuals strategize the screwing of other people by signing contracts (promissory notes) without having any intention of paying people back. 90% (estimated) of all big American companies, will go bankrupt, and fuck all their lenders, stock holders, bond holders, investors, etc. over the next 10 years. Ain't that awesome.

Most loans given to these companies are given by third party hedge funds, mutual funds, bond companies, and financial companies, which is money you have trusted to them for a long-term investment, such as an IRA, 401k, etc. They always loan and lose your money first that you invested with them. Their money is never lost for they control your money. You have a 99% (estimated) chance that this investment will become a nice gift at some point, and you will lose all your investment. I know that's not exactly what you intended to hear, but it happens every day in the new world of investing.

These fuckers, professional investors with their MBA's, will always lose your money over the long haul. The expenses and management fees, underwriting fees. processing fees, surrender fees, review fees, grab your ankle fees, will eat up any profits anyway, and you will be glad to receive ten cents on every dollar to settle all this bull shit once it's over. They will wear you the fuck out. 1% of you fuckers will have a nice ride and make millions, the rest of us, we are all just fucked.

Always let your investment advisor know that if he loses your money in some- kind- of- scam or something, that you will have to shoot them and then everything would be equal and that would be considered payment in full. That's how the Italians do it. It works every time.

Investment advisors, will think twice on how to invest your money, if they know they are going to die if they lose or scam away all your money. Always ask to see the financial advisors' portfolio first, so that way, you will know if they are full of shit, or they really do know what they are talking about. Most financial geniuses, have less than one month salaries in saving. How is this genius advisor going to manage my money, if they themselves can't even manage their own money? WTF.

Anything and everything that ends up in the bankruptcy courts hands, will most likely always become a gift. A good percentage of mutual funds, hedge funds, pension funds, 401k's today are all locked up from anyone making withdrawals. You may never see your money again. If your name is on the monthly statement, but you can't get your money, whose money is it really??? It's not yours, I promise. It's all bullshit. Remember, you can always sue those bastards. Good luck. Lol.

Do not loan money today to family, and/or friends. If you do, I promise it will turn into a gift, and you will never get paid. Today, a gift is money that you loan and never get back. It's that simple. Only give gifts or nothing at all. That's it.

Bankruptcies of large corporations, are mostly strategically planned. In America, the bigger your corporation is, the more debt that you have, the more people you fuck, the better chance you have of getting a government bailout (car manufacturers, banks, financial institutions, insurance companies, etc).

Little business guys like us? Forget it. Bankruptcy is a fantastic way to screw all your lenders, stockholders, investors and contractors, if you choose not to pay. It's also an acceptable practice in doing business today. This is sad, but it's life.

Many people have gotten rich by scamming and cheating their lenders, using bankruptcy and other legal tactics. Donald Trump, our Republican Nominee for the 2016 Presidential Election, is an example of a man that knows all the legal loopholes in the United States Bankruptcy Code. Moral of the story: never invest or loan money to anyone unless you are prepared to give it as a gift. All loans are considered gifts when not repaid and some are tax deductible, some are not. Got it?

Remember, if you are lucky enough to borrow money or sign a promissory note from individual or a bank, etc. Pay it back at all costs or don't borrow the money at all. No one wants to do business with people who don't honor their commitments. Be a good role model and pay your fucking bills the best you can. The system of credit will not work if everyone is a fucking crook. Fulfil your obligations. Got it? That was easy. How hard can it be to pay your fucking bills? Enough about bill paying, I think you guys are starting to get it.

66

Why Is the Stock Market A Big, Money-Losing Joke?

When the market is going up, yes you will make money; but what goes up, will always come back down. The important thing is knowing when this will happen. Ninety-four percent (estimate) of you, will lose your ass in the stock market if you're in it over a five-year period. You must have the inside trade information to make money in the stock market long-term. It's that simple.

Your broker's expenses, surrender charges, strategic planning charges, commissions, management fees, auditor fees, assistant to the manager's fee, assistant to the auditor's fee, and withdrawal service fees, etc. are all part of the stockbroker or financial planner scam. Brokers, will always tell you, it's a good time to get in the market, no matter if it's high or if it's low. When the market is high, and going strong, your stockbroker says it's a great time to get into the market, even though it's going to go lower. When the market is down, they say you can get in cheap. It's called dollar cost averaging, or goat fucking and it works every time. I love my broker, they are all geniuses, not. Most all stock brokers have net worth's of a shoe lace, go figure.

When your stock goes to zero, and you have done the dollar cost averaging bull shit like your super, fantastic stockbroker told you to, the value of your portfolio is still zero. That was a great investment. Ha-ha. WTF. It's all bullshit.

If you have money to lose, and you never want to see it again, give it to your stockbroker and kiss it goodbye. Who knows? You might get lucky and become one of the 1% of rich people by playing with stocks.

Always remember: what goes up must come down, and what is down may go back up. Airplanes always end up on the ground somewhere, and so will your investments. If you stay in the market long enough, over time, you will lose and get fucked. If you have millions of dollars to lose, it's all okay. Don't worry, be happy. Remember, if the yield is too good, and the promises are money-back guarantees, it's a scam, and you will lose eventually. It's just a matter of time.

Also, remember, that your financial planner, stockbroker, and investment advisor will never lose. Bernie Madoff was a fantastic example of a great financial advisor that fucked more people than any one person on this earth. You go Bernie, that fucker is a "genius". They always make a nice commission, and/or fee, and Bernie, is still alive. Holy fuck, are you kidding me?

Investing in today's world is all about inside trade information. Stockbrokers are big crooks who steal your money and tell you what you want to hear. They bait you with small bets, and get you hooked on larger ones, to steal all your money. If you do not have inside trade information, you will lose every time.

Ponzi, is another good scam. Ponzi investors get hooked on high yields that are all fake. New investors pay for old investors' yields. Eventually the Ponzi scheme collapses and all your money is gone.

Don't want to do that again. That was fun, not. If you are one of the lucky ones that get your investment back before the Ponzi collapses, you will still get fucked by the FTC. The FTC (Federal Trade Commission) will go after a bankruptcy claw back charge against you, and you will have to return all your money or go to jail. That's awesome. WTF. I forgot to mention the tax implications on this shit are through the roof. Stop that shit today.

Remember, your own bed mattress will never fuck you. Put real cash in safes, and/or in a safe place so it will always be there when you need it. Money at zero percent, is a good return, because the principle is still always there. I know you are losing to inflation but since we have no trust in the financial system, at least you won't lose your principle and get fucked.

Don't forget about the DEPRESSION in the 40's. It's coming again, and it will make the last one look like a little baby. The next one will be the big one, you won't need a bunch of money, but I would have a really big gun (AR 15) handy. With an AR-15 handy, you can always go get money. Got it.

67

Insurance, Annuities And Bank Scams

Insurance and annuities, in today's world is another scam. Insurance companies have $3 of liquidity (estimated) for every $100 of liability. Most insurance companies no longer pay their claims, and work like a Ponzi. The only way to get paid from an insurance company today is to hire a lawyer. That's sad. If you think you have insurance coverage, you will never know until you file a claim.

Annuities, are supposed to be safe investments, but they are locked and loaded with expenses for the brokers and insurance companies, and have zero guarantees for liquidity if they end up in bankruptcy. Insurance companies have minimal government guarantees and are insured by the broke state in which you purchased your insurance in. I feel better already. Broke times broke, equals broke. Have any question?

Insurance contracts, are supposedly guaranteed by the broke state in which the insurance contract was written. Most all states are broke, and can't even pay their own bills. Good luck trying to collect from a bankrupt insurance company, from the broke state your insurance contract was written in. Broke insuring broke – now that's fucked up. Are you feeling happy yet?

Remember, in life there are only two guarantees: death and taxes. Cash is always king. If you're looking for safe investments, I suggest you put all your assets into cash and find the best bed mattress that you can find. Your own mattress won't fuck you.

I know, I have already told you this, but I like to repeat myself just so it is crystal clear. Don't take candy from strangers, and don't give all your hard-earned money to strangers. They go hand in hand. Remember, don't give money to family members, even though they make fantastic, investment advisors, not unless you're giving it as a gift and have it to lose. Cash will always be king, enough said.

The banks, are another big joke in America. They are all broke. They all have scammed, look at Wells Fargo's fraud bullshit? They all have creative P and L statements to make themselves look good, so they can keep the FDIC out of their cooked books, etc. The banks, all use these creative accounting methods (called strategic accounting), and it always makes the numbers correct to the person they are trying to hose. They post future earnings ahead of time, they don't properly expense debits, and they strategically cram down their lenders. They cook all their books and nobody goes to jail for all this illegal activity here in America. This is some crazy shit. It's a party.

In some countries, when you scam and commit fraud, the CEO jumps off the highest building he can find and commits suicide, and this is considered honorable. These fuckers in America, they get a badge of honor, when they scam and commit fraud. As long as you pilferage enough money from your fraud here in America to pay your legal bills, you can jack off the legal system for years, and just pray you die before you might have to go to jail. That's right, nobody goes to jail for corporate fraud here in America. We send pot smokers to jail. That's fucked up.

CFO, CEO, COO, and shareholders must keep the fake numbers going, or the whole thing comes crashing down. Banks and securities companies, will be the biggest house of cards you will ever see crash in your lifetime. It's all your money, 401K, CD, Stocks, Insurance, Money markets, etc.

I hope the government remembers to get its big, fat check book out fucking fast when the banks start to fail, or we are in for a revolution right here in America. When the next war starts, do you want a pile of money or a pile of guns and ammunition? I will take the later. Just remember one thing, guns and ammo will always bring you more money, for you are in the driver's seat when holding an AR-15. It's the boss, got it.

The new fraud the banks are now using today, is they all have these brand new fake wills, that are supposed to save their ass in a down economy and/or if America is on the verge of a collapse. This bull shit will never work either, but they were told to do it, to make the American people feel more comfortable. I feel better already, ha. The banks charge us for every service they offer, and it's our own fucking money. They even charge us to hold our money. That's fucked up. Enough said.

If you are broke, and have no money, you are one lucky fuck, for you will never get fucked by the big, bad banks, and they will never lose any of your money, for you don't have any money. If you are a saver and have accounts in banks, watch out, the depression of 1929 is going to look like nothing compared with the depression of 20......... It's coming, be prepared. Cash in the mattress will never fuck you unless your home burns down. Put it in your mattress, (safe) that's better than FDIC today, and chances are your home will not burn down. Good fucking luck.

The banks have taken all your hard-earned money that you have given them for savings and checking accounts over the years, and lent it to a bunch of scamming corporations and big business (through triple A rated bonds and loans). These big companies have no means, and/or intentions of ever paying the money back and they will all go bankrupt eventually, anyway.

These big banks also buy big buildings for themselves, buy big airplanes for themselves, and pay big salaries to all their top people and fuck all the little people that makes the bank run. You know those tellers work their asses off for peanuts. It's kind of sad.

General Motors, a hundred-year-old company that knows how to go bankrupt the right way. GM fucked the bond and stock holders out of 200 billion dollars plus, and then borrowed from the same American people they just got done fucking. How many times can you have it shoved up your ass, people? General Motors knows, they had to be laughing the whole fucking time. Now that is genius.

Government Motors (GM), borrowed 60 billion dollars from the same people they just fucked. Are you kidding me? How is that possible? This is called a goat fucking in the 1st degree. It's a SCAM. Only in America can you pull this shit off and not get shot. WOWWW.

It is sad, but the way to make lots of money in America today is to borrow as much money as you possible can, as fast as you can, from lots of third parties. Then to complete the scam, steal all the cash from the business you possible can, buy a big gulfstream jet to fly around in, and then file for bankruptcy and tell all your creditors to go fuck themselves. That's how bankruptcy supposed to work in these United States of America, I guess. Does this sound like anyone you know? Donald Trump, do you know how this scam works? I know, you were just using the United States of America bankruptcy laws the way they were written to be used. I know you did nothing illegal. I got it.

Fraud is on the rise. Everyone at some point has been part of some form of identity theft, bank, stock, loan and or credit/debit card fraud. Less than 1 percent (estimated) of these scamming fucks ever get prosecuted, and basically no one ever gets convicted or goes to jail. Only in America.

Anything under 50,000.00 dollars never even sees an investigation. It should be first offense is on us, second offense they chop your left hand off, third offense your head comes off, then all the sudden, crime stops. Holy fuck, what a great idea, oh that's right, these douche bag attorneys will fuck all that up too and prevent any punishment to anyone. I forgot, everyone has rights, even if they are a mass murderer in America, fuck that shit.

Remember, the banks have $1.46 (estimated) cents in reserves for every hundred dollars of liability they have. What that means is, if more than 2 percent of you assholes want your money out of the bank at the same time, one of you assholes are going to get fucked, for it will not be there. Its probable invested in China or something. Good fucking luck trying to get your money from those guys over there. Let me know how that works out for you? Are you kidding me?

All banks bad assets are renamed and called current so it looks good on paper to the public. The next crash that is coming to banking, stocks, and financials will make all the other crashes put together look like they did not even exist. The latest scam in banking is charging the consumer to put money in their bank, now that is fucked up. Stick with cash, it will always be king.

Lastly, let's talk about the wonderful, scamming credit rating services, Standard & Poor's, Moody's, and Fitch Group. These fuckers are the biggest frauds on the planet.

They credit grade all your securities and financial investments with a bunch of numbers and letters based on how much you can pay them. Are you fucking kidding me? You are telling me, if I give you two million dollars, you will give my security a triple A rating, and now I can sell a fraud security to the average consumer and they are all fucked. Is that what you are saying? Oh, that is genius. Now that's fucked up.

When a company goes bankrupt with an A rating from one of these three, fantastic, credit rating agencies, they do what's called an" oops". Oops, is where you are being fucked and your money is now gone, and they are so sorry for your loss. We must have made a minor mistake in our calculations or something. This is the point where you call them, and ask them if they have been to the gun range lately; we should talk privately and work this all out, if you know what I mean?

You guys are starting to get it, right. If you have read this book in its entirety, you have learned more in the last two hours about women and finance than you will for the rest of your adult life. Now you can see why this famous book is the road map to survival in the 21 Century.

68

A Must Know—Rule Of 72

A very important investment rule if you have money and can find secure investments, "the rule of 72" is pretty cool. Take the interest rate of the yield on your money and divide it into 72. Example 10% interest rate divided into 72, will tell you how many years it will take you for your money to double.

In this example, your money will double roughly every 7.2 years (estimated). Say you have a $10,000 investment, and it has a 10% yield; you will have $20,000 in roughly 7.2 years. Wow, this is exciting.

This rule was taught by my grandfather when I was 7 years of age, and I have applied it throughout my whole adult life. I love you, Grandpa.

69

Government Is A Mess: Why Does Everyone In Government Lie?

Your government, is a train wreck that will eventually collapse under its own weight with all the lying, cheating politicians. No one tells the truth, everyone is on the take, and no one can get along because that's how you make money in today's world, by starting ciaos and creating drama. Don't get wound up in any political discussions, all you will do is lose your friends, and raise your blood pressure. It's not worth it. Fuck that shit.

Count your blessings every day if you are above dirt, and enjoy the freedom you currently have. You cannot fix all the world's problems. Don't put the burden on yourself to fix all the wrongs of the world. Live life to the fullest and just accept the world as it is—all fucked up—and you will live a lot longer. It's all okay. Your heart will love you, too.

By the way, I forgot to mention that health care is a bust and will never work. Get over it. Pray for good health, and take care of yourself the best you can. Quit smoking, drink less, exercise, eat good healthy foods, and I guarantee you will feel much better. In life, you only get one physical body. I never understood why people will punish their bodies, and not take care of themselves. Do one healthy thing for your body every day, you will be glad you did.

70

Employment Today

Employment in today's society, is a mess, due to all the litigation and bureaucratic bullshit. Most companies don't want their corporate headquarters located in America, due to liabilities and taxes. You will have an estimated 25 employment opportunities to get to the ripe old age of 65 in today's world. Your parents probably had just one job their whole life. They had benefits, pensions, health insurance, dental insurance, and vision insurance. That shit is long gone. Get over it.

Today's employment in America is a joke. It's mostly minimum-wage jobs in service or retail with no benefits, and everything today is pretty much all part-time or piecework. How are you supposed to raise a family in America with a job that barely pays above minimum wage? Good fucking luck.

TIPS FOR YOUNG PEOPLE ON GETTING A BETTER JOB

First of all, I am going to teach you young people how to prepare for a new job. Employers are burned out from your stupid, know-it-all attitudes. If you want a shot at a good employment opportunity, remember these six requirements:

1. Be on time with everything you do: Never be late. If you know it is going to rain, leave yourself plenty of extra time so that you're on time for work or any other commitment. It's called planning. You can always be early and start the coffee pot at your employers. If you are always late, just stay home and find a new job.

2. Dress Code: Remember, dress code is what your asshole boss says it is.

3. Drama check: Check all personal drama at the door before you walk into work. Customers and employees, do not need to hear all of your personal problems. All work-related issues are private and should never be discussed outside of work.

4. Be coachable, trainable, and teachable: If you are not on board with these three, you are fucking useless to your employer. I don't care how you were taught at your other job. You need to be able to listen, be coachable, teachable, trainable, and do the things your current employer wants done. THE END.

5. Don't know something? Ask your boss. If you don't know how something is done, or should be done, ask whoever is in charge, or your boss. Then do it the way he wants it done. You can make suggestions, but if he says differently, then just do it his way. It's that simple.

6. Lastly, have fun and make money. Working in today's environment is very stressful. Deadlines, projects, and equipment problems are all part of business. Budgets, goals and all of the above can make work seem everything but fun. Your goal is to do the best job possible, and have the most amount of fun doing it. This is a challenge, but do your best and you will prevail.

Remember, when seeking employment, you must find enjoyment in something that you like to do, or you will not be able to do it very long. For some of you, self-employment is the way to go. Being self-employed, is the hardest thing you will ever do. You now have no vacations and no paid time off; you are a bookkeeper, salesperson, project manager, and house cleaner. It never ends and the stress of paying all your bills, and meeting all your goals is through the roof when you are self-employed.

I have been self-employed for over 35 years and it has been very rewarding, but I have worked 80-hour weeks my entire life. Most people have never truly worked a 40-hour work week. Double this for 35 years, and you will be a little tired. If you decide that you can't work this hard, then self-employment is not for you.

If you are a technology person and have fantastic computer skills (coding), then by all means, start some kind of product or service business online. The name and tagline of your business is very important for it to get traction. Marketing your business is the second most important part of business for it to become profitable. If you have a great product or service, you will make money on the World Wide Web. Google, Facebook, Instagram and Twitter, combined with other social media and the World Wide Web—you could have a billion-dollar idea. Good luck, and don't let anyone steal your dreams.

71

Lease Your Car: Less Stress, And Cheaper

You never have to buy a used car ever again. Leasing is the only way to drive a car. Cars are expensive today to own, drive, and repair. The best way to drive a vehicle is to lease it (basically renting what you use). The reason leasing a car is so valuable is because driving a car outside of a warranty is absolutely stupid today. Transmissions cost upward of $5,000, and engines can cost over $7,000 today to replace. Air conditioning repairs can cost over $3,000. Putting this kind of money into a used vehicle does nothing to increase its value. If you lease a vehicle, almost everything is covered under the warranty while you are renting the vehicle.

Never put money down on a lease, for it is a waste of money. If you have good credit, you can lease a vehicle by making just the first monthly payment. When leasing a car, all you should be worried about is the monthly payment and the mileage restrictions and return fee. By not buying the car, you do not have a depreciating asset sitting in your driveway, and remember you're only paying for what you use for you do not own it. Renting or leasing is a lot cheaper than owning when you think that cars can cost upwards of $70,000 today.

If you're a high-mileage driver, you can purchase the car that you have leased over the period of years for the residual purchase price and have no mileage penalty, or negotiate the mileage away when you make the trade. More on that later.

It really does not matter what the interest rate or the purchase price is for all we care about is the monthly payment. Old people do not understand leasing, for their generation cars were not that expensive, like they are today. The monthly payment, is all that matters and you pay your states sales tax monthly instead all at once. It makes sense. Hyundai's, Hondas, Toyotas, Nissans, and Lexus's are the best for leasing, as they have the highest residual values, which gives you the lowest monthly payments.

Also, only shop for a leased vehicle on the last 10 days of the month. All dealerships are motivated to sell vehicles on the last few days of the month, for they have monthly incentive goals that they are trying to meet. Never go into a dealership without knowing, you are walking away on the first visit, and yes it does pay to shop around for all manufactures have certain specials and models that have the best deals for the month or week. Ask about those deals? You can never get the best deal on the first visit, let them call you back, so that the real negotiations can start working for you. Always start offering monthly payments $150.00 less than they offered you. It's a start. Remember, never any money down, that way you only have to compare monthly payments and mileage restrictions. Makes comparison shopping easy.

Last, but not least, always start looking for your new leased vehicle 90 days before your old lease is up. The reason you do this, is that it gives you negotiating power. The dealer wants to sell you a car today, so they may buy out your over mileage, they may wave or pay for your return fee. You may have equity in the lease and be able to use that to lower your monthly payment. The bottom line is to always start looking for a new leased vehicle before your backed into a corner and need a car that day. Got it. Enough said.

Never pay cash for a car unless you just want to pay for a $10,000 used buggy. Paying cash for a depreciating asset is foolish. Put your investments into positive appreciating assets, not automobiles. If you buy used cars from a dealer or at an auction, you must be super careful. Some of these cars have been drowned in water, have had major vehicle accidents, or have had poor maintenance. Don't get stuck with a lemon. They're expensive. Always do a Carfax on a used automobile before purchase. Remember, if a car has been wrecked, and/or repaired, and paid for in cash, it will not show up in a Carfax report.

Some mechanics are crooks; they all love to work on your vehicle. Most can't fix anything, but they sure know how to screw up everything. When leasing a new vehicle, you have simplified your life, for you don't have to know a mechanic. You don't have to worry about previous damage, flooded vehicles, or poor mechanical repairs. All you have to do, is make the monthly payments, drive and get the required service. How simple life can be when you're in control and you don't screw it all up.

Mechanical breakdowns on used vehicles are a nightmare. You might have to be towed, and you might not have control of the towing company, and/or the mechanic shop. You have to take time off work, and you have no vehicle to drive. Just lease a vehicle and I promise you, your life will be easier. That was easy.

72

Home Ownership Is A Pain In The Ass: Rent vs. Own

Homes and cars are pains-in-the-ass, and both are very complicated and expensive today. In the past, it paid to own your home and the vehicle you drove. Today, the world has changed. Buying real estate has made people rich over the past centuries. Lately though, real estate has become a Debbie Downer.

Let me explain: today you purchase a home for you and your family. It comes with an expensive mortgage payment, expensive insurance, expensive taxes, expensive homeowner's dues, expensive plumbing repairs, expensive roof repairs, expensive air conditioning repairs, termite damage and sinkhole possibilities. All of these expenses can bankrupt your family and put you in the poor house for the rest of your adult life. Going to work every day, just to pay for all these home expenses is not fun. Rent. That was easy.

It pays to rent. Somewhere in the last 20 years, it has become less affordable to own your own home. Long-term, renting is the only way to go. It's just the opposite of what your grandpa would say.

You only have to worry about two things when it comes to renting: paying your landlord and checking to see if the home you rent from your landlord is in foreclosure. Checking to see if the home is in foreclosure is easy to do, if you have a computer. All *lis-pendens,* (foreclosures), are a matter of public record in the county you reside in.

The other reason that owning a home is a pain in the ass, is that there is no job stability in America. If you are 25 years of age or younger, you will have at least 25 job opportunities before you get to retirement age. You will have moved at least 10 times, all across the country, and you will not be able to afford all the real estate commissions and closing costs that you will have to pay to sell all your homes.

The one thing about renting is that you have an easy escape if you must move for employment. You notify your landlord when you're leaving. That's it. Have a nice day.

Life is short. Don't be married to your home. The repairs and maintenance will make you tired, exhausted and broke. Let your landlord deal with all the repair nonsense; it's not fun. Got it?

73

College Is Not For Everyone

When you were, a kid growing up, you never knew what you wanted to do for a living when you got older. You have had all of these life experiences. Your father might have been a policeman, accountant, etc. Your mother might have been a nurse or teacher. You watched them struggle and juggle with employment, family, and now it's all about you. You have finished high school and now the real world is about to begin. Holy shit. WTF.

What the hell are you going to do? You are going to take all your life experiences and this fantastic book that taught you everything about women and finance, and use all this knowledge that you have acquired and become a productive citizen. At least now you know what you are getting into. Before this book, you had no clue. Look what you have learned so far! If only ten percent of this information that you have learned from this manuscript is ever applied to your life, just think how much easier your life will be. You are one, smart S.O.B. You and your lady have been educated beyond your wildest dreams.

For most of you, college, is the first time you have ever been on your own. You set your own schedules, plan your meals, have part-time jobs and try to figure out what you're going to do with the rest of your life. If you want to become a doctor, lawyer, or engineer, etc. you must complete many classes and graduate to get your degree. A four-year college degree can cost over $200,000 today. Find your passion and work at something that will make you happy, and I promise you will go far. It's never too late.

74

Parents, Get Over It: I Am Not You

For those of you like me, college looks to be no fun. You have options, too. You can go to a trade school to learn a skill, such as air conditioning, trucking, electrical, plumbing, auctioneering, or whatever your heart desires. Some of you have no people skills, and are very immature for your age. Some of you have researched small business opportunities and you may want to start your own business: landscaping, auto repair, construction, etc. Don't just talk about it; grow up and do it. Step up, and be a man or woman, grow some balls, let's go.

The moral of this story, is to find something you enjoy and just do it. If for some reason, you go to college because your parents want you to, and you decide on a career that you hate, you will be one miserable person. Find something you enjoy and all your employment issues are solved.

Remember, you're only here on this earth for a blink of an eye, so be sure your employment brings you joy every day. I have a friend, who is a fire-fighter and he loves what he does. I also have a friend, who is a plumber and he hates what he does. Do something that you love and the money will come and you will have a very fulfilling life. That was easy.

75

Life Insurance

Life insurance companies are in the business to make money, and it is very complicated for you to understand their fucked-up programs. Life insurance is very simple. Never buy a life insurance policy that combines a death benefit and some kind of savings product all in one. This could be called universal life, variable life, whole life or permanent insurance, etc. Who the fuck knows what scam name they call it today? These bundled products, are all rip-offs, and are very expensive unless you are a high net worth individual.

The only insurance that you need for insuring one's life is term life insurance policy. If you die within the term of the policy, the company will pay your beneficiary a death benefit. It's that simple. Your insurance salesperson will always try to sell you a combined savings and death benefit (bundled policy), because he or she will make a lot more in commissions. Don't ever combine a savings or cash value account with a life insurance death benefit—you will always get screwed.

Also, no one needs permanent insurance for his or her entire life. At the end of your life span, do you want a pile of insurance that you can't spend, or do you want a pile of money that you can spend? I would choose the money. Let me explain. The most insurance you will ever probably need, is when your last child is born. The day your last child is born is your biggest financial support day in life, and it decreases daily. Kids never need to own life insurance, except possibly a burial policy. Children don't support anything and are not obligated to pay any bills.

All the combination policies are scammed to steal your money with high premiums and they pay low death benefits vs a simple term policy. Don't do it.

When buying insurance, always shop around for an A-plus rated company, even though the ratings are all a scam, too. Ratings can all be bought with money, so they have very little financial value. Most insurance companies today don't pay their legitimate claims without you hiring an attorney anyway. Disability insurance, if it is available to you and affordable, can be very helpful if you become disabled. It will replace 60% to 80% (estimated) of your income if you're hurt or injured and you can't perform your duties at work. Shop around for the lowest premiums because they vary quite a bit.

Now, that you have learned about insurance scams that combine savings with life insurance policies, you will better understand why it is so hard to get an agent to sell you a low-cost term policy to protect your family. Buy a low-cost term insurance policy and invest the difference. I also suggest that you start a monthly savings account for emergencies and retirement. Fifteen percent of whatever you make, should go into a secure account CD (certificate of deposit), or something that is 100% safe and is Federal Deposit Insurance Company, insured. You should always have an emergency fund for unexpected expenses. We know your money won't grow with these products and you're losing to inflation, but at least the principal amount can never go to zero and lose money like stocks and other investments.

Today, all retirement funds need to be 100% safe, so as not to be lost in this scamming market. Remember, the only guarantees in life are death and taxes. That was easy. A good financial planner can help you with all your insurance needs. Always be sure to get three opinions and shop around. That was easy.

76

Wills Are A Must

Wills, are something that everyone needs but are rarely used. A proper will is an instrument that tells the world how you would like your shit distributed after your lawyers, judges, and family have fucked over your estate. A will, is another document that gets litigated if your family members don't agree with your wishes.

Lawyers, love these documents and can't wait to get all your loser relatives fighting over all your shit, until there is no more money or assets (shit) left to steal. When the lawyers have sucked all the money out of your estate, they disappear like flies.

Between the lawyers, the IRS, estate taxes, state income taxes and inheritance taxes, there is little left anyway. Don't worry about what happens to all your shit after you're dead; it doesn't really matter anyway. Live life to the fullest every day and spend it all.

When you're dead and gone, does it really matter who gets your shit anyway? I don't think so. Enjoy life every day. Once you're dead, someone else can worry about your shit. It does not matter who fucks you over, after death. It's OVER. Don't worry about it. Not your problem anymore. THE END.

77

You May Need A Trust

A trust, is another instrument that offers great financial planning, if you become a millionaire. Contact your financial planner, and/or an attorney regarding the appropriate use of a trust and when it is needed.

Your bloodsucking attorneys, love to talk slowly about these complex financial documents. The average attorney charges $500 per hour to give advice regarding trust documents. Who wouldn't want to talk slowly about how they can put your assets into a trust? Your attorney has now created a billable hour scam that will never stop fucking you. This is genius.

Remember one thing: If your trustee dies, and your successor trustee dies, and the beneficiary is incapacitated or the trustee will not do the instructions the beneficiary has requested, you can kiss your assets goodbye until the wonderful attorneys and the court systems decide your fate. You will spend thousands of dollars on attorney fees, just to get your shit back from the fantastic trustees, that you trusted, once they are all dead—if you can ever get it back, at all. It's all part of the billable hour scam. Fuck that shit.

78

Keeping Up With The Joneses

In life, you will have pressure to keep up with the Joneses. You will want to have a bigger, more beautiful new home, a newer car, the bestest of furniture, the best clothes, a country club membership, etc.

Over time, you will realize, all this expensive shit is a pain in the ass. Don't get tied up with all this bullshit. Relax, chill, have fun, and always remember to rent everything. Life is fantastic if you enjoy the little things in life. Don't worry about keeping up with the Joneses. Enough said.

79

Be Sure to Count Your Blessings Every Day

Be sure along the journey of life, that you count your blessings: your true friends and family. Most families have issues; most of my family has issues all over the map. They're rude, disrespectful, ungrateful, have drug issues, and are thieves but in the end, I have forgiven all of them for their bad behavior. I cannot be the judge or jury of their lives. Remember, you can only influence people in this life, you cannot change them directly, just take care of yourself. That's it. It's all so SIMPLE.

If you ever have the chance to go out West and see the mountains, the rivers, the sunsets, etc., be sure to stop for a moment and smell the coffee. In life, you are going to have good times and bad, but always remember to be thankful for what you have. We are only here on this planet for the blink of an eye. Enjoy every minute of every day.

Don't stay mad at someone, or hold any grudges against him or her. I know it can be hard to forgive everyone who has trespassed against you (screwed you, fucked you over), but if you don't, the only one it will hurt, is you. Every day when I get up is a fantastic day, because I know one of these days I won't wake up. Live life to the fullest every day, and forgive everyone along the way who fucks you. Keep it simple, stupid (KISS). THE END.

80

Animals Are Man's Best Friend

Cats and dogs are man's best friends. If you have an animal, then you know what I mean. Let's say you have a rough day at work? You come home to screaming kids and a bitching wife. You can always depend on your pet to love on you. It's that simple.

Animals, always show affection. They lick you and hug you, when everyone else is being nasty and can't give you the time of day. Animals also lower blood pressure and bring your heart rate down. Animals don't smoke pot, they don't do drugs, they don't get drunk, and they don't talk back. I love my animals.

Now, you can see why kids are a pain in the ass compared to animals. So, next time your family is being ugly, disrespectful, and/or ungrateful, throw a bone to Fido, or pet your pussycat and let him or her be your best friend. Animals will never ever let you down. I promise you that!

Now, I know why men like to always walk their dogs. They do this so they can get away from their crazy female bitches that drive them nuts all the time. Remember ladies, men only need booty and respect, and everything will be just fine. That was easy. Men, don't forget to give emotional support and listen to all your lady's needs. Be kind, be respectful, and always treat your lady like a queen, if she is deserving of it. Got it.

81

The End

Now, that we have come to, "THE END" of this book, you as a male understand all the workings of a female, enjoy the ride. Men, have learned all the fucked-up dating "rules" that women are using in the 21st Century. Guys, I just want to say that dating and finding a good woman that will take care of you and your family, is kind of like you finding snow in Florida in July. It ain't gonna fucking happen. Good luck, have fun trying and never give up.

Women, have been taught, "the rules" of dating in finding a man to marry. These rules that they use are all fucked up ideas that some great, fantastic writer has put in their minds and now has fucked up their little heads. Women, if you're listening, quit being manipulative, dishonest, deceitful, conniving, and/or using trickery. Us guys today, know all your fucking games and we don't give a shit anymore.

Ladies, if you play all these stupid games with us, guys will treat you like shit and move the fuck on. Got it? Ladies, the thing that your rule book forgot to tell you, is that if you don't call us back when we call, make us wait when we stop by, or don't appreciate us and are ungrateful for what we try to do for you, we move the fuck on and we will fuck all your sisters and their girlfriends. How do you like those rules, bitch? Fuck your rules.

Ladies, stop your fucking games and all your scheming nonsense. We men have caught on to all your tricks and your vindictive ways.

The game is over, ha-ha. Not funny. Ladies, don't forget, the world does not always revolve around you, even though you may think it does. If you have learned anything from this book, it should be this: you can always become a better person and you can change your evil ways. Your man will always forgive you for your bad behavior, and you can have a fresh start. Now that us guys know all your stupid rules to finding a good man, the cat's out of the bag, you win.

Ladies, if you want a healthy, committed relationship, just be yourself. If we as gentlemen like you, we might pursue you. If we don't, we move the fuck on. The problem, when you're not honest at being yourself is that we don't see the real you until later in the relationship. Once we find out who you really are and we don't care for you, we are gone and we have both wasted time in our lives that could have been spent trying to find the right person.

Guys, like we discussed earlier, you're only here on the planet for the blink of an eye. Enjoy every date that you have. Have fun, work hard, go fishing, watch sports, drink beer, and be grateful for what you have. Remember ladies, all guys in your eyes will look like players, because we have limited time to sort through all you wonderful, fantastic females. Once we find the one girl who grabs our attention and meets our needs, we settle down and can be committed. Ladies, you need to do the same.

Guys, all ladies are fucked up at some level. You must find the least fucked up one who makes you happy. She should be compatible with your lifestyle, and you should both share the same interests and be able to get along. Ladies remember, all guys are fucked up at some level, too. It just takes a little longer for it to come out on boys and be seen.

When you do find a female or male relationship that works for you, be grounded, be committed, be respectful, be grateful, be appreciative, and always treat her like you would want to be treated, for someday it will all be gone. I wish you peace, love, joy and happiness for the rest of your adult lives. Remember, life is fantastic if you control it.

Lastly, common sense is a form of narcissism, in the opinion of other people that don't use or have any common sense. Read this last sentence twice, and it will start to sink in. If you have no common sense, you think everyone around you is narcissistic. This is totally untrue. People with no common sense, need to get their head out of their ass and wake the fuck up, and realize every common-sense person is not a narcissistic fuck. We just don't act stupid like they do, and we take control of our own lives and do not blame everyone else for our faults. It's that fucking simple. Because of this book, you are now educated beyond your wildest dreams and ready to tackle the world.

For all the men, boys, and ladies who have read this book, I know you have been enlightened. You now have read the #1 book in the world for fixing relationships. You now know everything there is to know about men and women in relationships. Men, you realize you are not the only one that thinks the way you think. Guys always ask themselves, why is my girl so fucked up and I still love her? Guys, it's called life.

If you can fix your relationship with the one you love, and be happy, good for you. If you are miserable every day, get the fuck out and find a new piece of ass. Yes, it's expensive to get out, but the price of being miserable every day is death to the heart and soul. You will become numb and miss out on all the good things in life if you stay with some person who makes you miserable, or who is miserable themselves. Remember, there is someone out there for everyone. We just have to find the right person for you.

When it comes to women, men, and people, I have a suggestion that makes it so much easier to deal with all of them. Lower your expectations of all your acquaintances, and friends to below zero and you will never become disappointed again. This sounds a little harsh at first, but in reality, by doing this you have lowered your blood pressure and nothing will ever bother you again, and you won't ever be disappointed again. That was easy. Let me show you how this works!

So, the next time your girl, and/or friend lets you down, you will not be disappointed with either of them, because you expected less than zero from them anyway, and that's what you got, they delivered. By doing it this way, you are not a narcissistic fuck and you can enjoy every day above the dirt. There is no more shock factor, for you expected nothing and you got nothing. Every once-in-a-while, somebody will do something right, and surprise the shit out of you, but don't have a heart attack, it's not going to happen often, don't worry.

Life, is so much easier this way. You will never be mad anymore, when you don't really give a shit. This works great with kids, parents, your boss, and your employees. These people will always let you down. It is what it is, move the fuck on. Look at the value of what you just learned here? Its priceless, now go out and apply this new concept and look how much more relaxed you are. It works every time.

Your family and friends will think you have lost your mind, when they are not seeing a reaction from you. I promise you, by doing it this way, you are not the same person you once were ten minutes ago. Live life to the fullest every day and never let these people disappoint you again. That was easy.

Getting back to finding that right person. There is a dating site out there for singles, where you can meet like-minded individuals who need booty and are looking to find love. Everyone needs booty.

Dating sites today have become very popular and are always worth a try if you're looking to find a new relationship. You must start somewhere, so why not try a dating site to meet new people? Dating sites are so much better than the bars, for you get such a broad selection of people to look at. Internet dating sites is where it's at today.

I hope this book has inspired you and that you now understand why things in life function the way they do. For the women, out there, who have snuck a preview of this book, be kind to your boyfriend or husband. Most of the time, your man is doing all he can to support and provide for his family. I hope that by reading this book, women have learned that men will go to the ends of the earth fighting for their woman if they get booty and respect. If you can't give your man these two things, then this relationship will never make it long term.

So, ladies, be sure to take care of your bodies, keep yourselves up, exercise, eat right, dress for success, and always look your best. Make your man proud to be with you and always be supportive. Your man will always love you if you can be nice, be grateful, and be respectful to him. Don't forget that he needs booty three times a week, without you bitching or nagging about something he did wrong. Life is short, so enjoy the ride. Men, you have do the same.

As we explained, finding a good woman can be very difficult, just like finding a good man to take care of you, is. The Italians, have the car door test that they always use on their ladies to test to see if she could be a keeper, or a throwback. It's pretty awesome and it works every time. Next time gentlemen, you are out with your girl, open the car door for her and let her into the car, and then close the door. If your girl reaches over and tries to open your door on the other side of the car for you, she might be a keeper fish, for she now is showing signs that she cares about you and the world is not all about her.

I love those Italians; they think of everything. So, guys, be a gentleman and see if your girl can pass the car door test. It's a small test, but it shows she cares.

And gentlemen, always remember to open the car door for your lady, as long as she appreciates it. If she is ever ungrateful, then just let the bitch get her own fucking door. Another problem solved. That was easy. Colonel Smoke, (The Master) knows all the answers regarding women.

Remember ladies and gentleman, always be the best you can be. Be sure to enjoy your family and friends every day. In life, you only go around once, and it's a very short ride. So be careful, learn from your mistakes and always stay focused on your dreams. If you're facing difficult decisions about a man/woman, and/or life skills in general, this book is for you. If you want to know the truth about dating, family, kids, sex, and life scams, this book is for you. If you have a friend who is thinking about getting married, or in the middle of getting divorced, get them this book immediately, and suddenly everything about relationships and life will become crystal clear.

All Men Are Stupid is a life changing, pull-no-punches, tell-it-like-it-is book. You thought you knew everything and realized after reading this book, that you had no clue. Don't allow any man/woman - or anyone for that matter - to change who you are, and/or steal your zest for life. Live life to the fullest every day, and don't forget to rent everything along the way. It's the only way. Life is fantastic when you take control of it.

Tell all your friends what you learned today. This book may never become a best seller, or be discussed on the Oprah Winfrey Show, Howard Stern Show, Maury Povich Show, Jerry Springer Show, Doctor Oz Show, Steve Harvey Show, The View, Ellen DeGeneres Show, Tonight Show, David Letterman Show, Jay Leno Show, Arsenio Hall Show, Don Imus Show, Rush Limbaugh Show, Dr. Laura Schlessinger Show, Glenn Beck Show, Nancy Grace Show, Neil Boortz Show, Erich "Mancow," Muller Show, Michael Savage Show, Tom Leykis Show, TMZ, CBS Network, ABC Network, NBC Network or FOX Network, but we gave it a hero's try, trying to explain all the emotional and irrational behavior of women to men.

This manuscript is written solely by, Colonel Smoke, (The Master) and is all about the truths and opinions of life experiences he has had. The knowledge and material gained from reading this book, will save every young man, and/or woman hundreds of thousands of dollars and headaches over a lifetime.

When I was young, if I had known what I know today, about life, women, and children, I would have worked less, vacationed more, and reserved more time for myself to enjoy the things that I wanted to do. Don't let the world control you so that you're stuck in a rut and trapped in a hole and financially broke. Read *the #1 book for fixing relationships* today, and take control of your future tomorrow. Always remember: never let any family members or friends take away and spoil your dreams.

Ladies, if you have read our book, start taking better care of your man, TODAY. It is never too late. Women, we applaud you for taking the journey with us. Now you know what all of us men know about women and how we think. You now can become a better person to your male companion. You have learned so much by reading this book. This would be a great time to evaluate all your issues (it's never too late).

If you become a better wife or girlfriend from reading this book, then our mission was successful, and we are glad you are here. Men, all these same principles apply to you, too, so be kind, and treat your woman like the beautiful lady she is.

If you only get one positive thing from this book, that means you have learned something. Learning to communicate is key to growing in a relationship. Hopefully, All Men Are Stupid has taught you to stop being nasty, stop being ungrateful, stop being disrespectful, stop bitching all the time, and everything here forward, will be just fine. This goes for both male and females, for its not healthy in any relationship.

This book was written to open your eyes to facts that you might not have been aware of regarding men and women. By improving your attitude and becoming more positive and understanding of each other, your relationships can only grow and become better. Men, really are not stupid. We try to support and take care of our families every day. We work hard, we play hard, and most of us bust our ass daily to support the kingdom that we started. So, ladies, that being said, let's make the best of what we have, and enjoy every day we are six feet above the dirt.

Men and women have fought for this country for years. Mostly men, have been on the ground and in the air, fighting, killing, arresting, securing, protecting American people on the front line. These men do these great things for only one reason, and that is to protect the American people from the bad people of the world. These men bust their ass, live in tents or camps, they have no running water, they have to shit in buckets or on the ground, it's cold, rainy, blowing sand and dirt, snowy. It's a shit life, but these great men do this every day without question.

So, ladies, the day you women take over the front line of real war and fight for our country to protect the citizens of the United States of America like these men have, then at that time, you have earned the right to be a nasty, miserable bitch to the men of the world. Until then, go fuck yourself. Be nice, be respectful, and be grateful to all the men of this country that have saved your ass so you can still run around and be a nasty, miserable bitch, if you choose, too. Put that in your pipe and smoke it, bitch.

The men of the front line, I want to thank you for your service, your sacrifices and your dedication that you have given each, and every one of us that live in these United States of America. Some of you are just now returning home from your duties and have been injured, maimed, killed and possible in need of all kinds of long term care. Ladies and gentlemen, we need to take care of our veterans at all cost, and help, encourage, treat and heal them the best way we know how. Some of these men have paid the ultimate price with their life on front-line war fair and their families are hurting badly. If you ever see a military person in the community, buy them lunch and thank them for their service. It's the least we can do for them.

The moral of the story is, until you have fought on the front-line, ladies, you do not have any right to be a nasty bitch to the men of this world. Got it. For the ladies that have been on the front line, we thank you. Let's take care of these men and women the best we can.

Women, don't forget to act like a lady and men will treat you like a lady. The problem in today's society, is that most women want to act like men, be paid like men, do the work of men, and then be treated like a lady. Fuck that. Women, want everything to be equal. Well, I'm here to tell you that if you want to be equal to men, the system of men treating you like a lady, but you acting like a man, will not work.

Remember, if you want to be treated like a lady, be sure to act, talk, walk, and look like a lady. It's all so easy if everyone just does what he or she is supposed to do. Life is short. Enjoy the ride and always do your best. That was easy. THE END.

Men, be sure to take good care of your woman and treat her like a queen if she has passed the, "Exclusive Keeper Test," designed by, Colonel Smoke, (The Master). This "test," will be the best investment to finding out if you have keeper, or a throwback. Our, "Exclusive Keeper Test Edition" is amazing, and has never been done like this before. Consider yourself lucky, you now know and understand, "the keeper test" and how it works.

The "keeper Test", when working properly, will test all your female's emotions. Your woman might get nasty, she might get ugly, she might throw the book out the window, she might throw the book into the garbage, and/or she might even set this valuable, informational book on fire. Holy shit, the truth hurts. If any of these happen to you after your women has read the most powerful book about relationships, she has got to go. She is no good. She did not pass the, "keeper test". Throw her the fuck out immediately and go find some new ass. That was easy.

This book is made to help men and women with relationship building. Now, after reading All Men Are Stupid, everyone understands everything about relationships, your women should be kinder, nicer, and more attentive to your needs if she is a true "keeper". You are a very blessed man. Remember guys, this test works both ways, so be sure to set a good example for the rest of us men. Got it.

Couples argue all the time about shit, that in the big picture, is no big deal and does not mean shit. Stop that crap, it's not healthy. Ladies and Gentlemen, my advice is, if you don't have something nice to say to each other, then shut the hell up. That was easy.

Colonel Smoke, (The Master) explains everything in this book on how life should work. Both females and males should read this book in its entirety, together. By doing it this way, everyone will have a few things they can work on together. If your partner always has to have the last word, then your relationship might not work. Be happy every day and find joy in the all the small things in life. I promise you this, if you follow our instructions, your life will be more fulfilling and enjoyable than it ever was before.

Colonel Smoke wants to thank each, and every one of you that has taken the time to read the most powerful book on relationships ever written. Now, you truly do know everything there is to know about men and women and relationships. Go out and share this book with every couple you know that is struggling and can't seem to get along. You are now an expert in this field, anyway. So, lets help everyone we can, today. GOD BLESS all of you. Keep the faith.

About the Author

As the author of this book, I want to get something straight. I do not have anger issues with women. I am not mad or bitter towards women. Women, who read this book, will tell me that I am angry, and/or that I hate women. No, this is not true. I, myself, love all women. The problem, if you will, is that guys can't understand the wiring of women and I am trying to expose all their circuitry (wiring if you will), so as to understand these female, walking hormones.

Now, that we have established that men are from Venus and women are from Mars, and women are complicated beings, that do not come with an instruction manual or service manual, that is understandable to men. We men, must decide if this intricate, fine-tuned, powerful machine is too complicated for us. A man's instruction manual as we explained, is very simple: booty and respect. So, if you are a woman, remember: we men are just trying to figure out all your irrational behavior and put it towards our best use, since we now know we can't change, and/or fix our females. We now understand, that we have to deal with it, if we are going to be attached to someone who is of the opposite sex.

We as men, just have to make a decision, to find out if the value of joy and happiness, outweighs the pain and expense that we must endure with this relationship. Women, you need to analyse the same thing at this point, it's only fair.

If you have a pussycat that you live with, that has two legs and is cute and funny, but is nasty, you can trade her in for a four-legged one, that will just purr in your ear, hug on you and will never talk back. Your pussy problems have been solved. That was easy.

So, ladies, if you have read *All Men Are Stupid,* hopefully you have will apply the 101 plus guaranteed ways to a happy relationship with your man. Please, don't be angry with the author, your man or yourself, if you really want to make your relationship better with your significant other. You can always change and work on improving yourself, so as to become a better and more understanding person.

Now, that we have explained how men and women are supposed to act, anything less than this from here on out, is considered disrespectful. Guys, you can only tell your women so many times how things should be done. It sad, let it go. If your woman is going to be disrespectful, ungrateful or just plain nasty, it's over, just get the fuck out as fast as you can. You as a man, can only try to fix shit so many times, after that, we are done.

Hopefully, your man or woman has passed the "keeper test" with flying colors. For those of you that have failed miserable, we wish you luck in finding your next relationship. Remember, with every new relationship, you are starting from scratch and you have a new beginning on life, so be kind and always be respectful.

On the other hand, Gentlemen, if your women has passed the, "keeper test" with flying colors, always be kind, treat her with respect, and be sure to show her how much you love her every day. She is part of the 1% club. You are very blessed. Also, ladies, if you decide your man is a keeper, then give him all the booty and respect that you can muster and I promise you both, you will have a fun fulfilling life of happiness with no regrets. The End.

This book, to all women will hit a nerve, for it is, a relationship information book that women have a hard time comprehending. It's a little over the top, but I promise you, you are a much smarter person today than you were before this book. So, ladies, look what you have learned, and be proud of yourself for now you know how to keep your significant other happy and healthy, until death do us part.

Be yourself, (don't be fake) when you're with your man. This makes it much easier for us to decide if we want to be with you. It also saves lots of time if we get the "real you," immediately. Everything is so simple in the real world if people just act like themselves. By reading this book, you can always change your evil ways and become a better person. It's never too late.

Now, that we are at the end of this book, if you have any questions, concerns, or comments regarding your woman, please contact "Colonel Smoke," at Allmenarestupid.com. Colonel Smoke, (The Master) has cracked the code, and knows everything about women and men, and now that you have read this book, you do too!

In closing, I would like to give a shout out to all the police, fire, armed forces, and security personal that keep us safe in America every day. The freedoms that we share, are because these men and women work diligently every day fighting for our safety and security. These people are what make it possible for us to go about our business every day.

So, next time you see one of our public servants in uniform, buy them a meal and thank them for their service. By doing this, you have told someone how much you appreciate them and it will make you feel like you have done something good at the same time. Be kind, be respectful, and always do something good for someone every day, and I promise you, you will grow as an individual and be a much happier person inside. It really does work.

Now, that you know everything there is to know about life when it comes to relationships. Go out and try your new 101 plus guaranteed ways to a happier relationship, and never be disappointed ever again. You now have all the tools and understand why things are the way they are. All you must do, is apply your new acquired knowledge you have learned from the one and only, Colonel Smoke, (The Master) and your life will become so much happier and easier. I guarantee it will, if you follow all our proven techniques that we have discussed in this book. Go get'em tiger.

Read – *"All Men Are Stupid"* today, and start living a more fulfilling and happier life with the person you love, tomorrow. The END.

Colonel Smoke,(The Master)Trunk Test
The Trunk Test

Everyone needs a dog or cat. Your pet will never let you down. You will find that people and families can be nasty, rude and will always let you down and disappoint you. In life, you work all day and when you come home you must deal with all the issues of your wife, girlfriend, and/or children, but your dog and/or cat, no matter what, are always excited to see you. Dogs are loyal, loving, and just want to be with you.

Wouldn't it be nice, if your wife or girlfriend's attitude toward you, was like your dogs? Do you remember the story about the dog, the female, and the car trunk? Well, here it is. Lock your dog and your female into a breathable trunk. At the end of two hours, open the trunk and see which one is happy to see you; then you know who truly loves you. Your dog is always happy to see you. Your female, on the other hand, will be pissed off. Go figure. Your dog licks you to death, sits in your lap and walks by your side, your lady will bitch until your head falls off.

Ladies, I already know what you're thinking. NO, we don't want you ladies to be our dogs, we just want you to act and listen to us like our dogs do. That's it. It is so simple.

One percent (estimated) of you gentlemen, already have something special with your lady and you know who you are. Be grateful every day and count your blessings for what you have. You have something that the rest of us all want. We, on the other hand, have our dogs and cats, and are thankful because they love us unconditionally every day. We love our animals. Life is fantastic with our pets.

Testimonials

Booty and respect is all we need. *Colonel Smoke, hit* the nail on the head and is 100% correct. Thanks for opening our eyes to relationship building and communication. We got it.
Bill and Lynda Y.

All Men Are Stupid, is a must-read for all adult males and females. Grow some balls gentlemen, and let's take our lives back. I love the, "keeper test". My girl, did pass!
Sammy D.

All Men Are Stupid, is all about becoming a real man in the 21st Century. You saved me from getting married. My bitch went crazy when she saw this book, she was not a keeper. Your test works great. Colonel Smoke, you did me a favor. Thanks
George F.

This book explains everything about women that I need to know. My wife and I of 29 years agree with 95% of everything that you said. Best investment I ever made. Now, we all know it all. Thanks for the education, Colonel Smoke.
Bozzy and Kathy B.

Free Prenuptial Agreement

_____, hereinafter referred to as Prospective Husband (GIVER), and _____, hereinafter referred to as Prospective Wife (TAKER), hereby agree on this _____ day of _____, in the year _____, as follows:

1. Prospective Husband (GIVER) and Prospective Wife (TAKER) contemplate marriage in the near future and wish to establish HER respective rights, and responsibilities regarding HIS income and property, and HIS income and property that may be acquired, either separately or together, during the marriage. It's all bullshit.

2. Prospective Husband (GIVER) and Prospective Wife (TAKER) have made a full and complete disclosure to each other of all of HIS financial assets, as more fully set forth in HIS accompanying Financial Statements, attached hereto as Exhibit A. She wants it all.

3. Except as otherwise provided below, Prospective Husband (GIVER) waives all HIS rights, and agrees to the following screwing:

    a. To NOT share in HER estate upon HER death. Just give the bitch everything.

    b. To support HER pain-in-the-ass children from previous marriages.

    c. To NOT share in the increase in value during the marriage of HER separate property. She is the boss.

    d. To GIVE 100% of his pension, profit sharing, or other retirement accounts to her. Bitch wants everything of course.

    e. To pay 100% of all legal, and court fees for both parties.

    f. To pay any claims based on the period of cohabitation of the parties. Give it all up for pussy.

4. [SET FORTH RELEVANT EXCEPTIONS HERE.] She gets everything.

5. The Prospective Wife (TAKER) agrees that the Prospective Husband (GIVER) be deprived of continual and ongoing sex WHENEVER he requests, the Prospective Husband (GIVER) shall be granted full permission to shop at an open store.

6. Both Prospective Husband (GIVER) and Prospective Wife (TAKER) can be represented by separate and independent legal counsel of their own choosing, but the Husband (GIVER) must pay for both scamming attorneys, and all legal fees. (makes sense).

7. The Prospective Wife (TAKER) will have separate income or assets, and will milk the Prospective Husband (GIVER) for everything. Sure, why not, makes perfect sense.

8. This agreement constitutes the entire agreement of the parties, and may be modified only in the disappearance of the Prospective Wife (TAKER). Prospective Husband (GIVER) will agree to report her missing within 6 months. Lead Poisoning disease or whatever.

9. In the event, it is determined that a provision of this agreement is invalid, because it is contrary to applicable law, that provision is deemed separable from the rest of the agreement, such that the remainder of the agreement remains valid and enforceable. She deserves it all. SCAM.

10. This agreement is made with the knowledge that <u>GOD GIVETH and WOMAN TAKETH AWAY,</u> and any dispute regarding its enforcement will only be resolved if the Prospective Husband (GIVER) pays for it. That was easy. Bitch is expensive.

11. This agreement will take effect immediately upon the solemnization of the parties' marriage on this date. _____ What the fuck.

I HAVE READ THE ABOVE AGREEMENT. I HAVE TAKEN TIME TO CONSIDER ITS IMPLICATIONS. I FULLY UNDERSTAND ITS CONTENTS. I DON'T AGREE TO ITS TERMS BUT WILL SUBMIT TO ITS EXECUTION BECAUSE SHE WANTS TO GET MARRIED. I HAVE GOT TO BE STUPID. SEX STOPS ON MARRIAGE.

* Consult an attorney to be sure you're being screwed

_____   _____
Prospective Wife (Taker)   Prospective Husband (Giver)

NOTES:

Made in the USA
Coppell, TX
10 September 2022